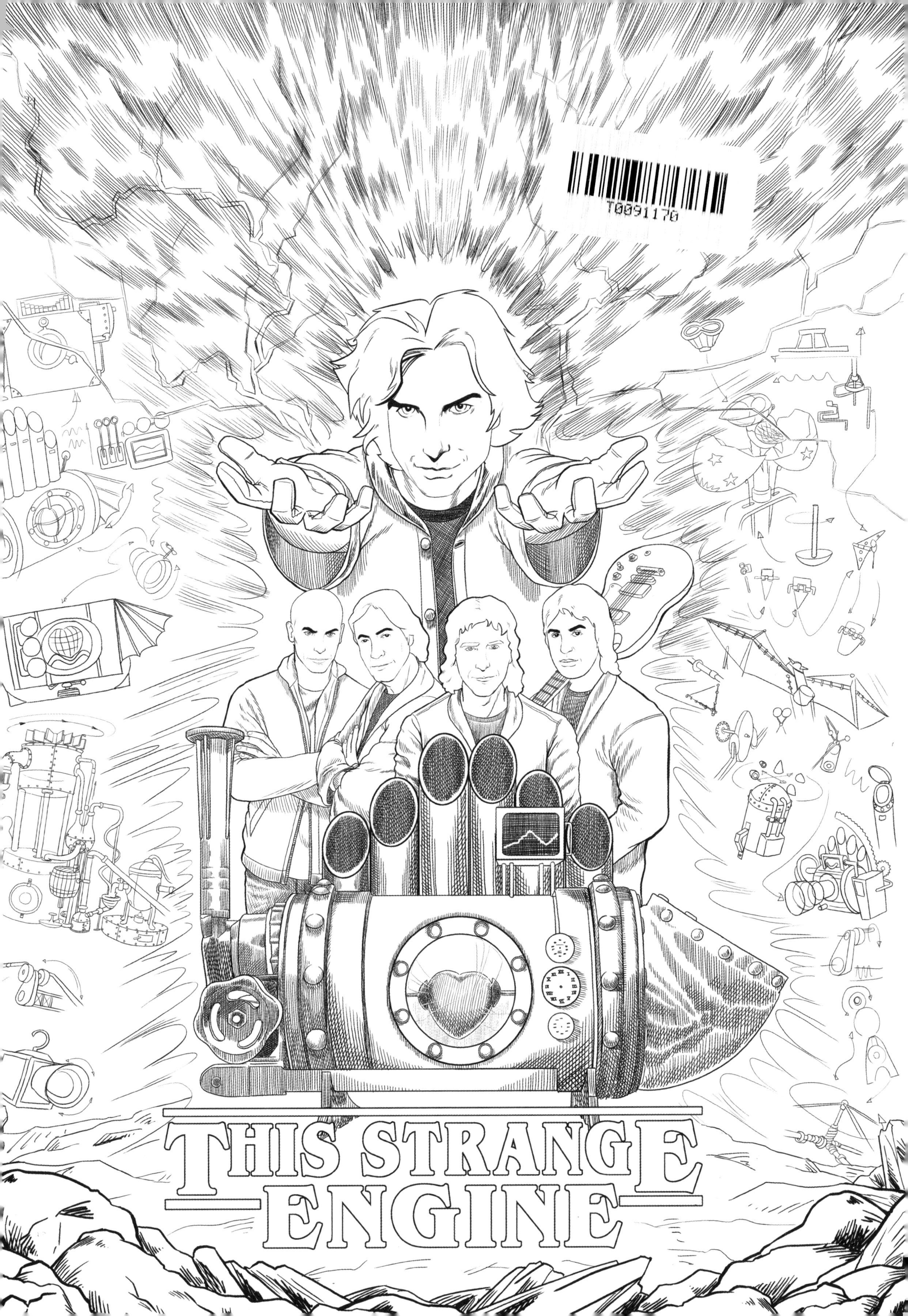
THIS STRANGE
ENGINE

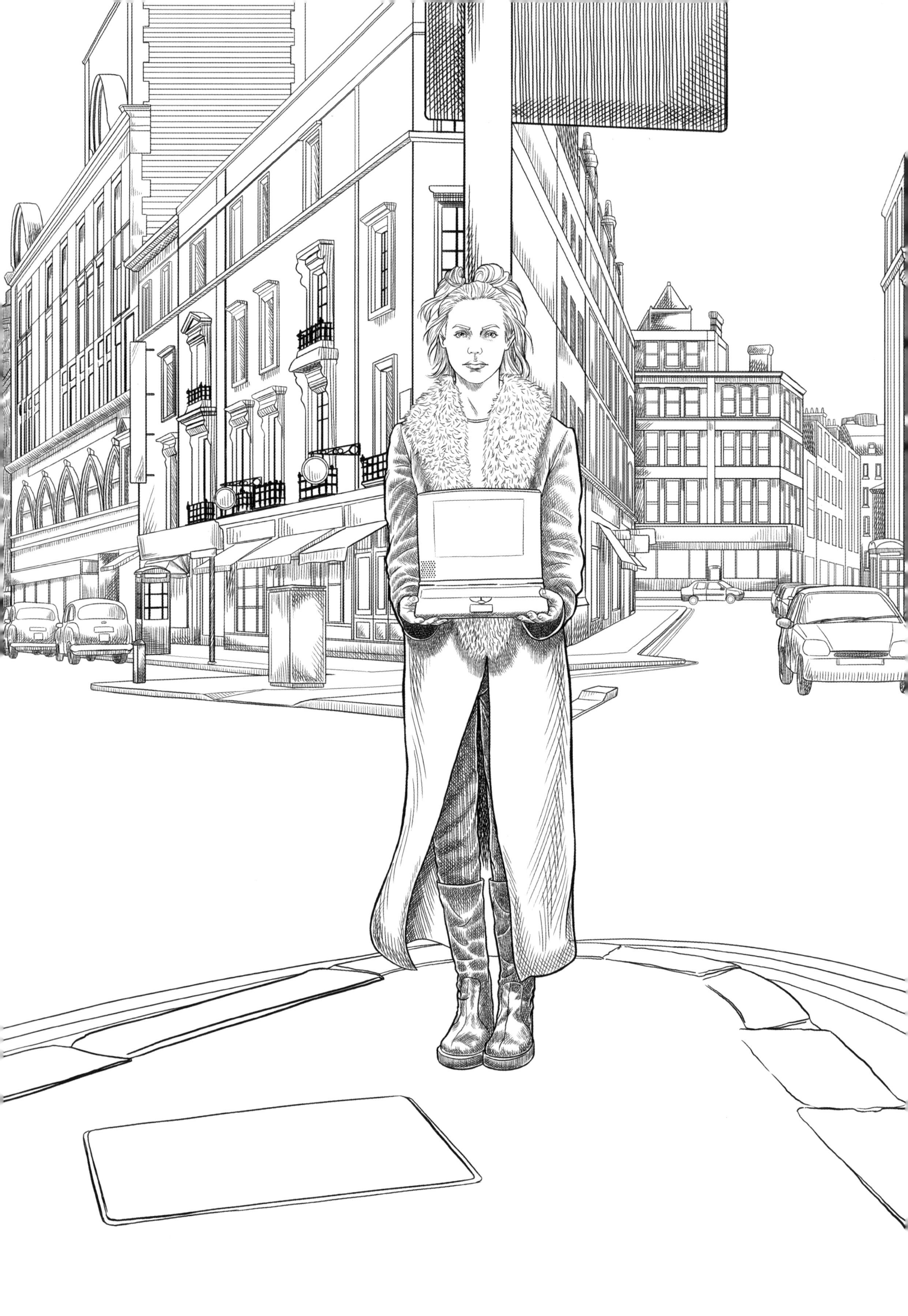

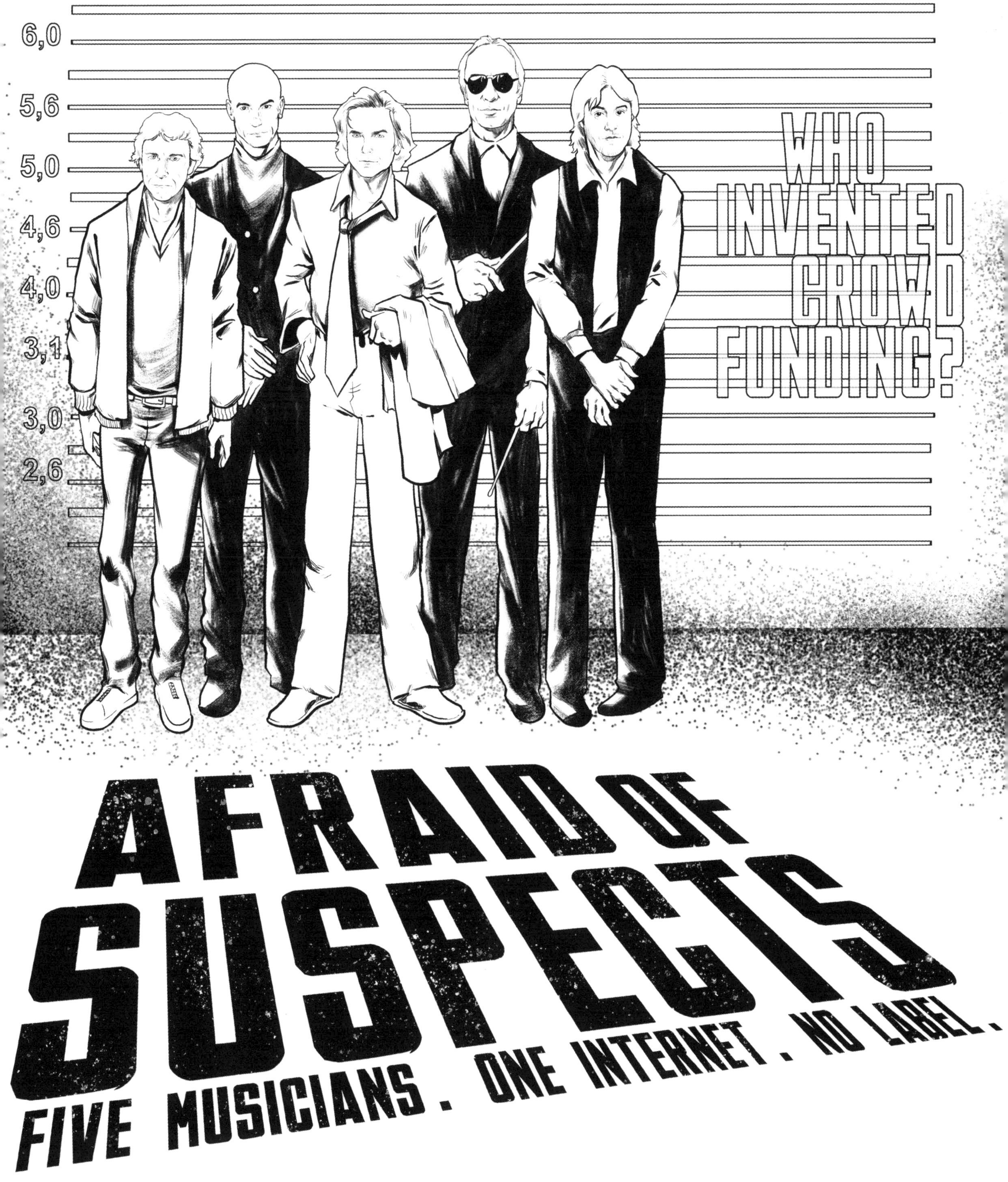
6,0
5,6
5,0
4,6
4,0
3,1
3,0
2,6
WHO INVENTED CROWD FUNDING?
AFRAID OF SUSPECTS
FIVE MUSICIANS. ONE INTERNET. NO LABEL.

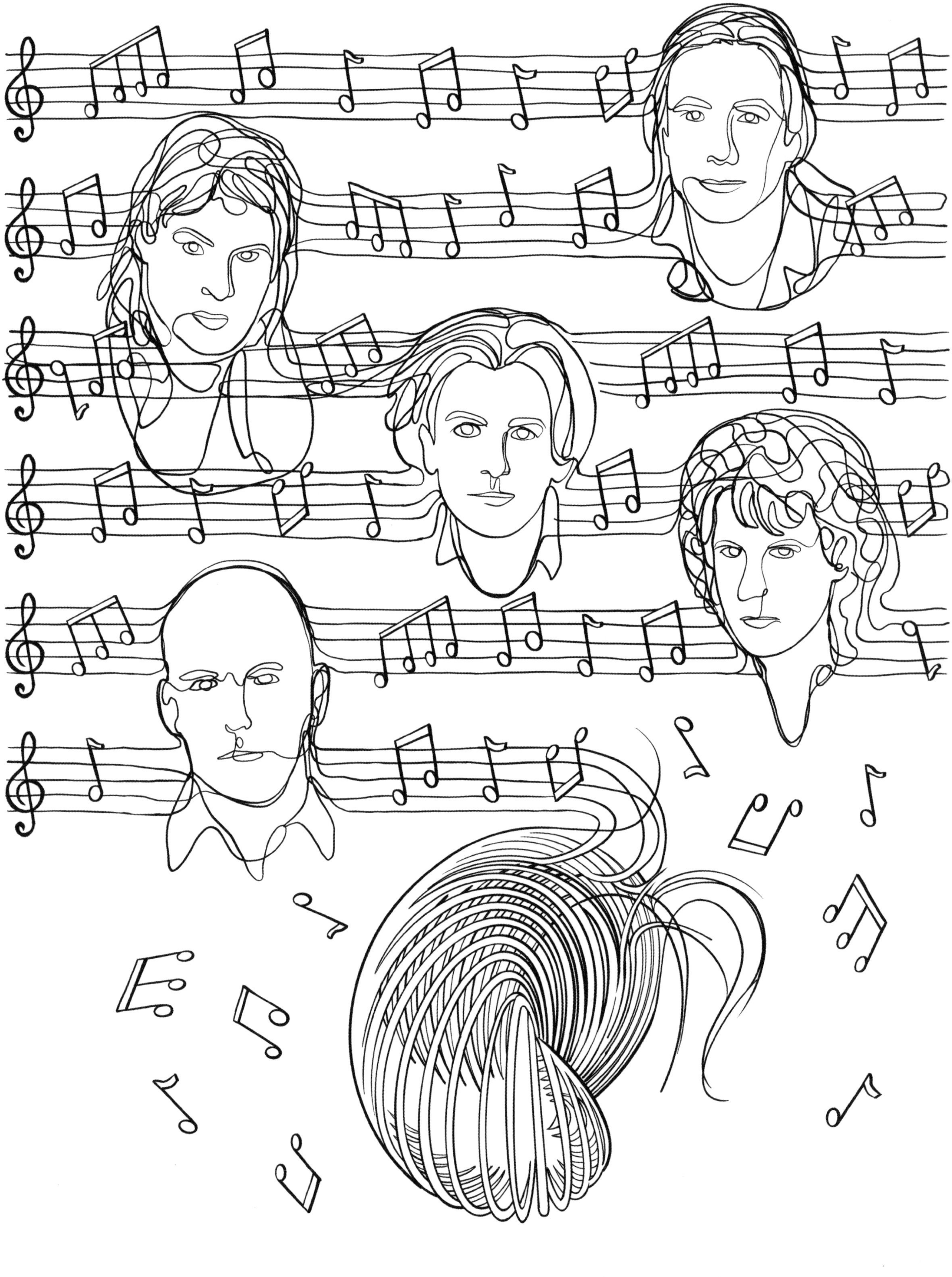

MARILLION SOUNDS THAT CAN'T BE MADE

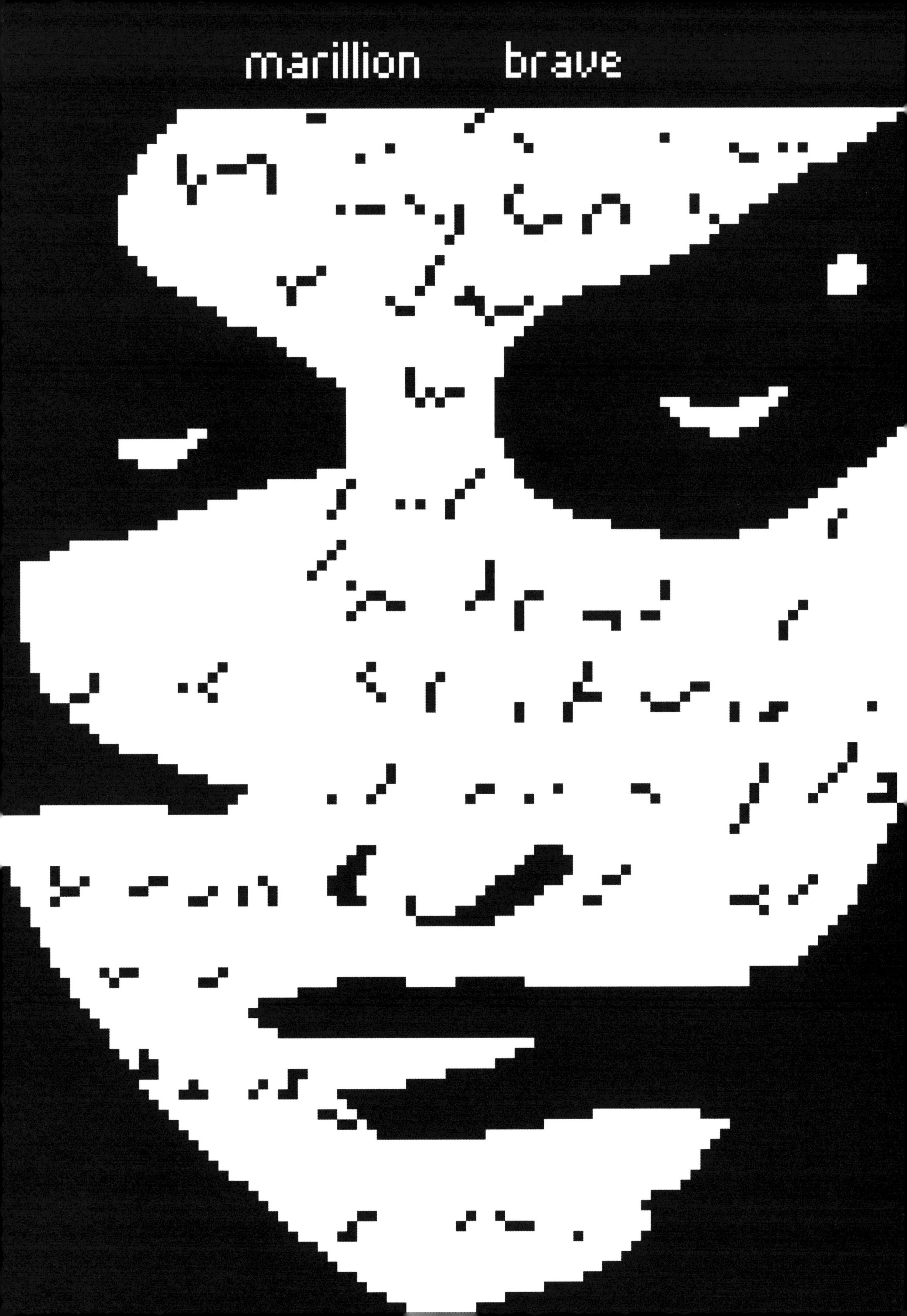
marillion brave

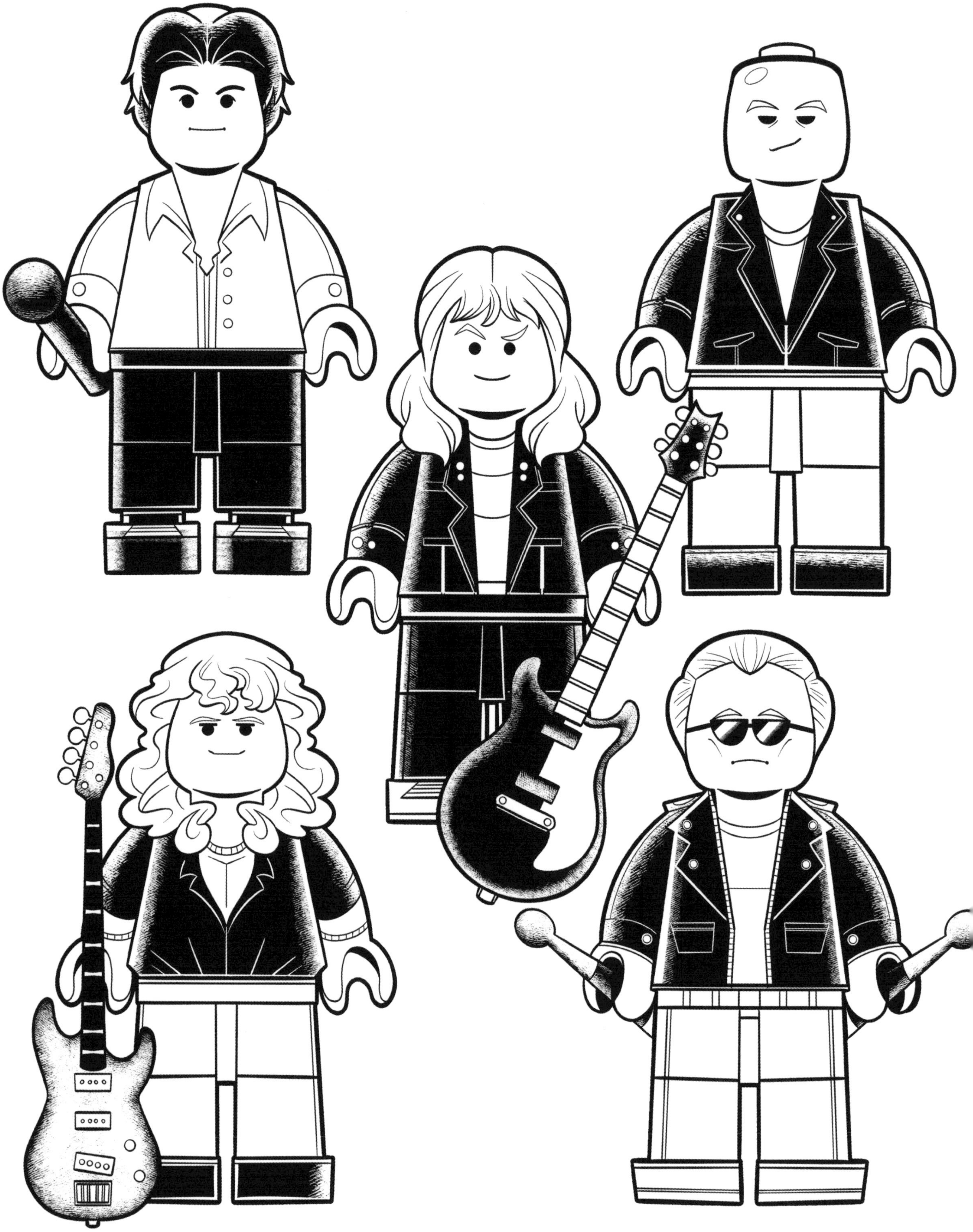

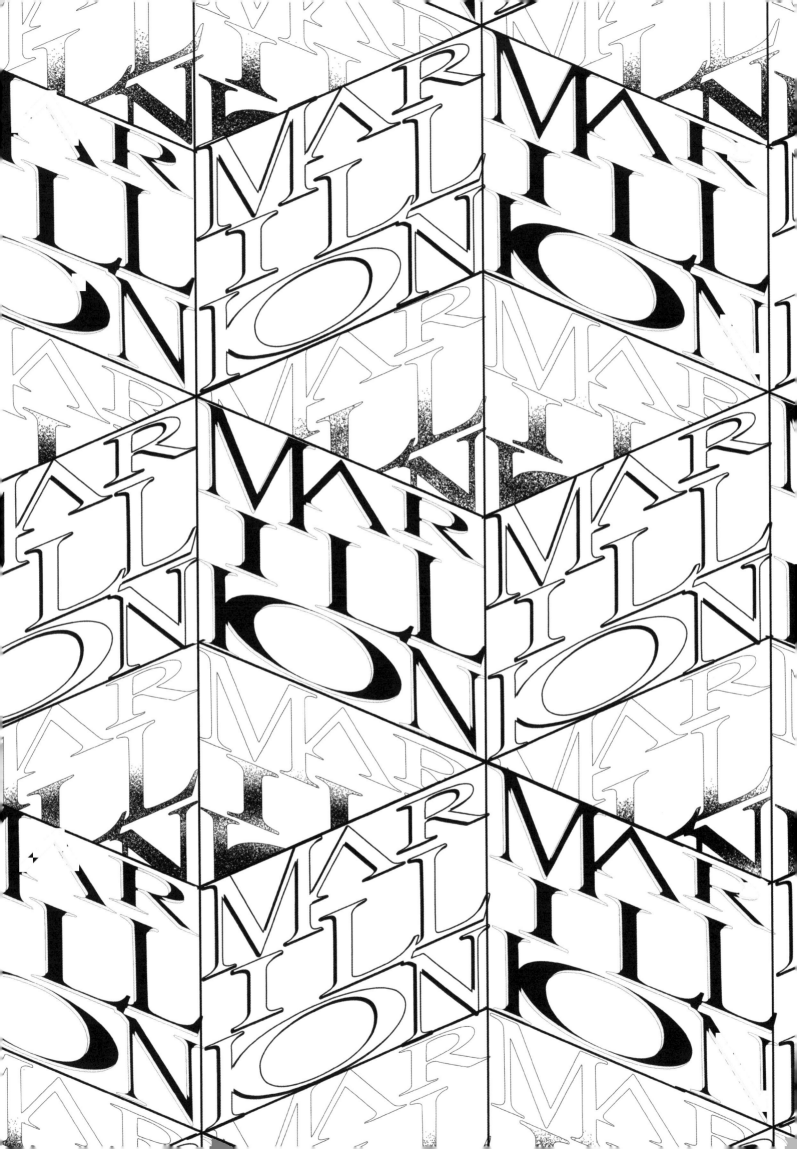

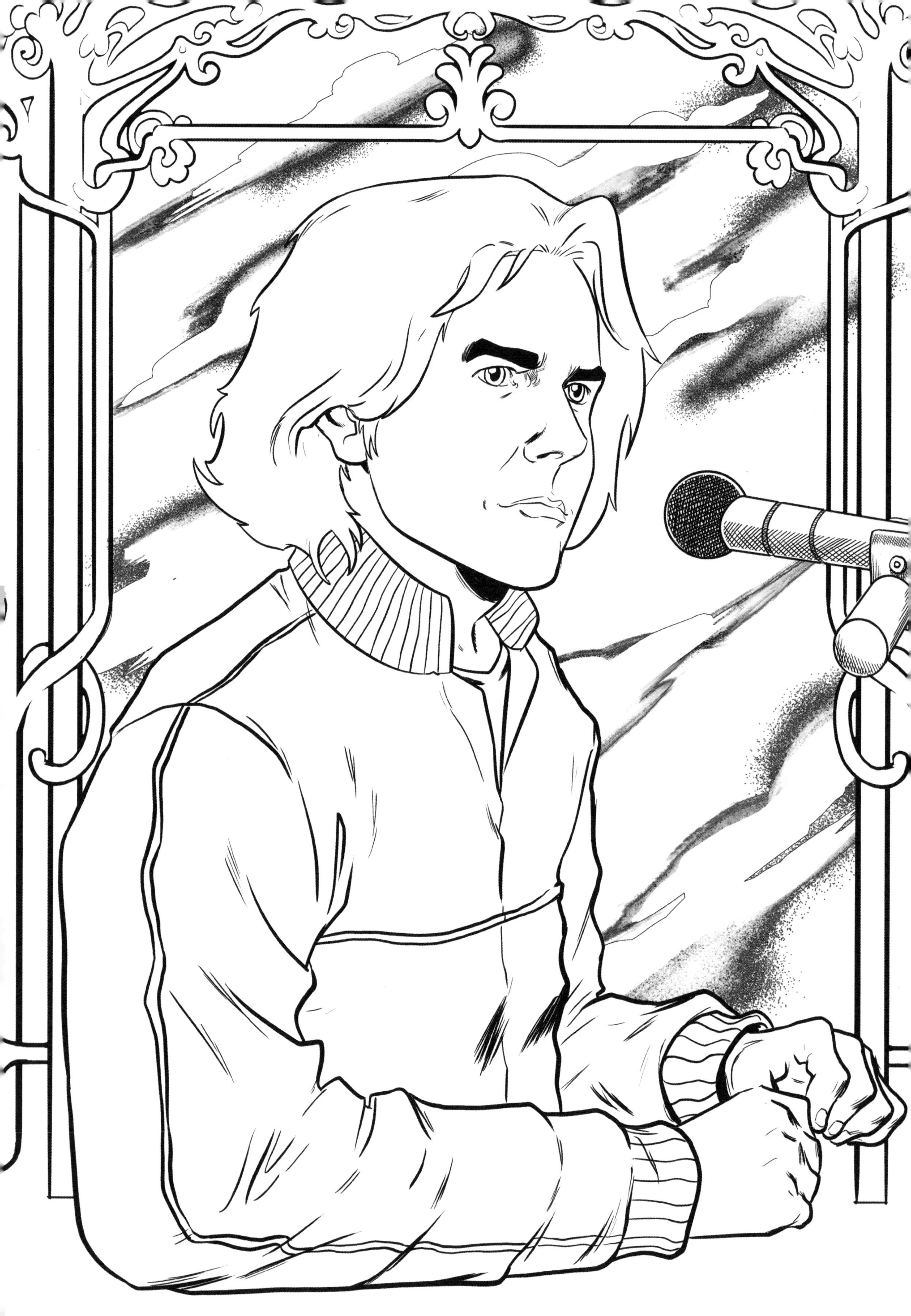

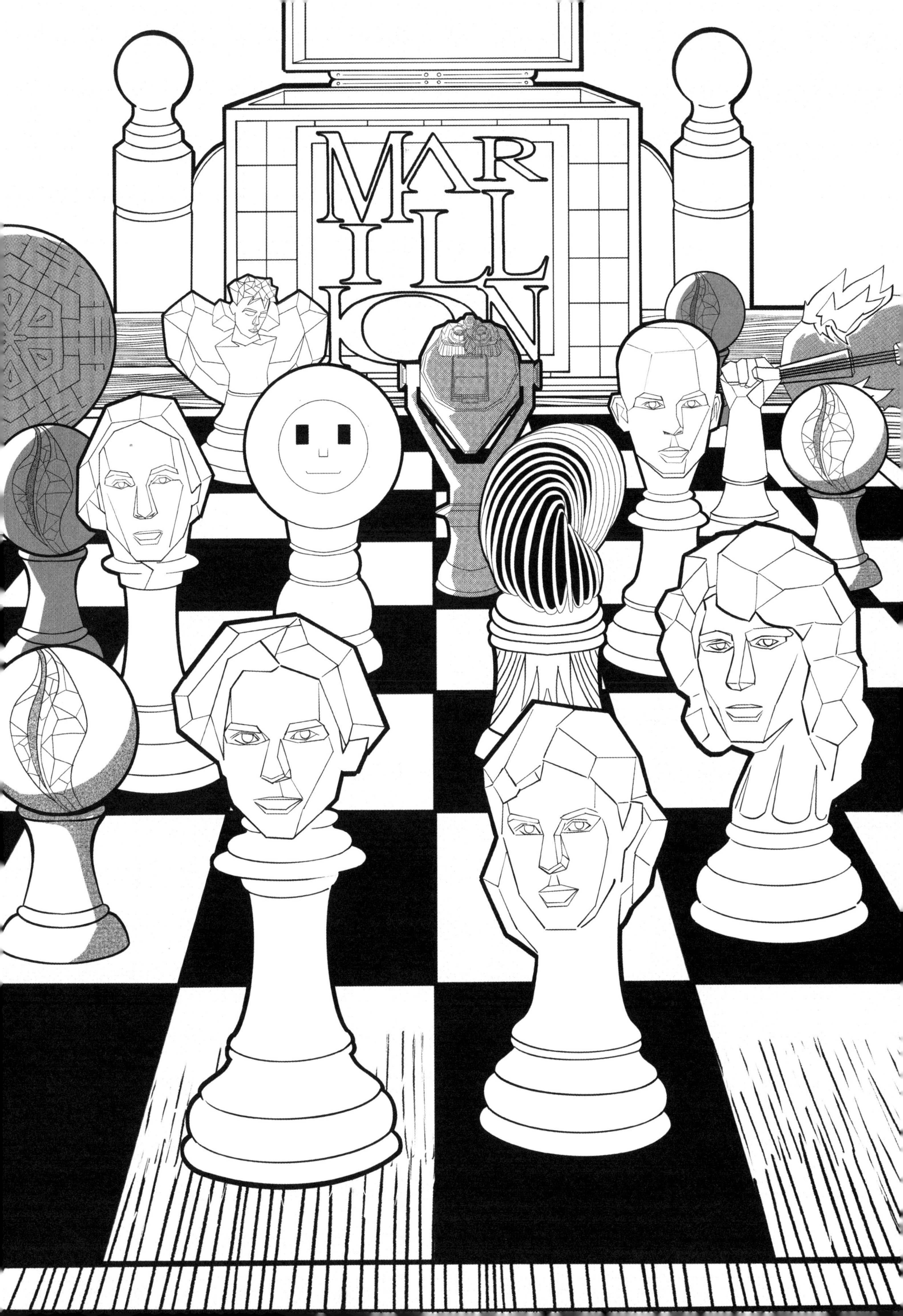
MAR
ILL
ION

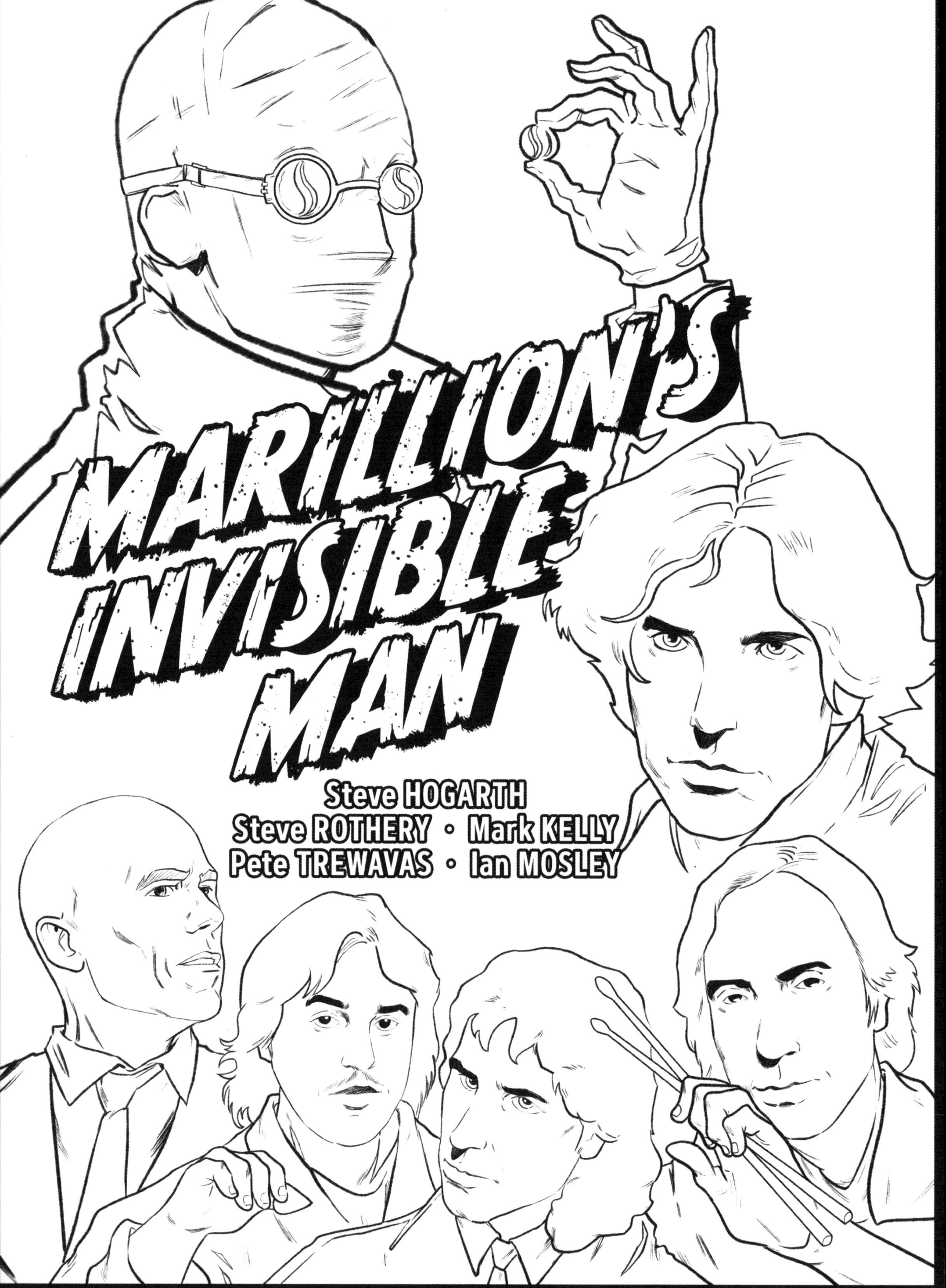
MARILLION'S INVISIBLE MAN
Steve HOGARTH
Steve ROTHERY • Mark KELLY
Pete TREWAVAS • Ian MOSLEY

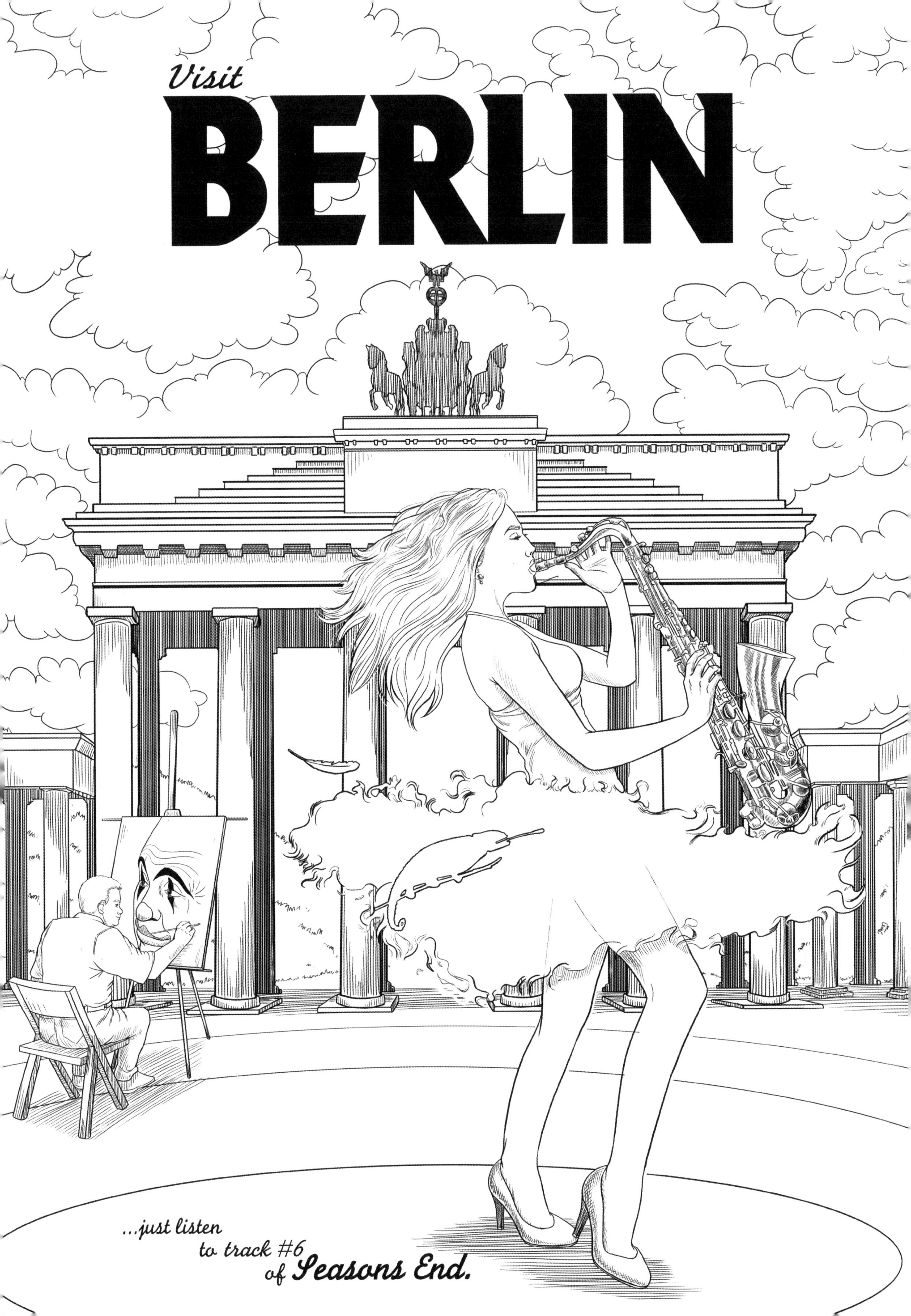
Visit
BERLIN
...just listen
to track #6
of Seasons End.

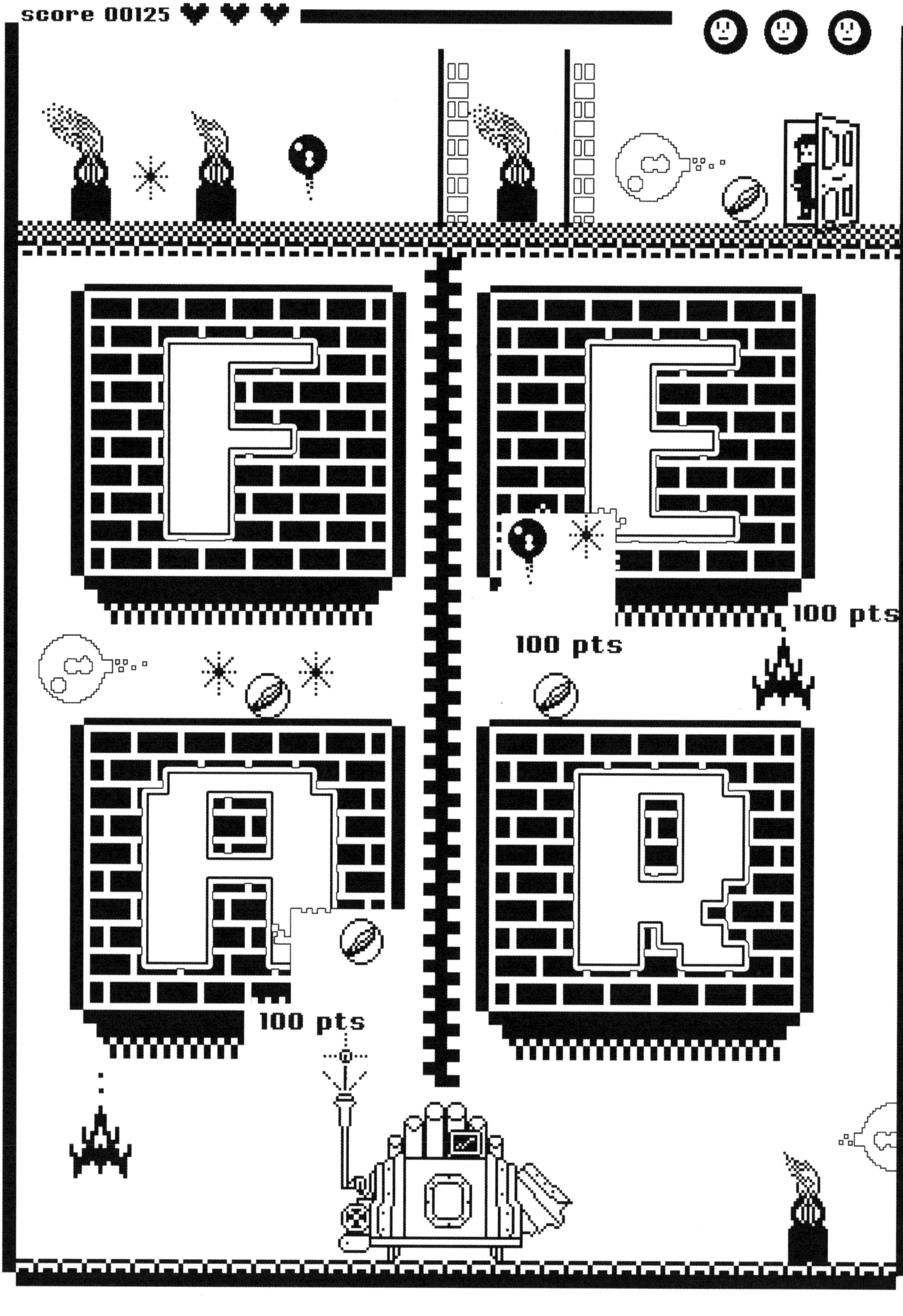
score 00125
F
E
A
R
100 pts
100 pts
100 pts

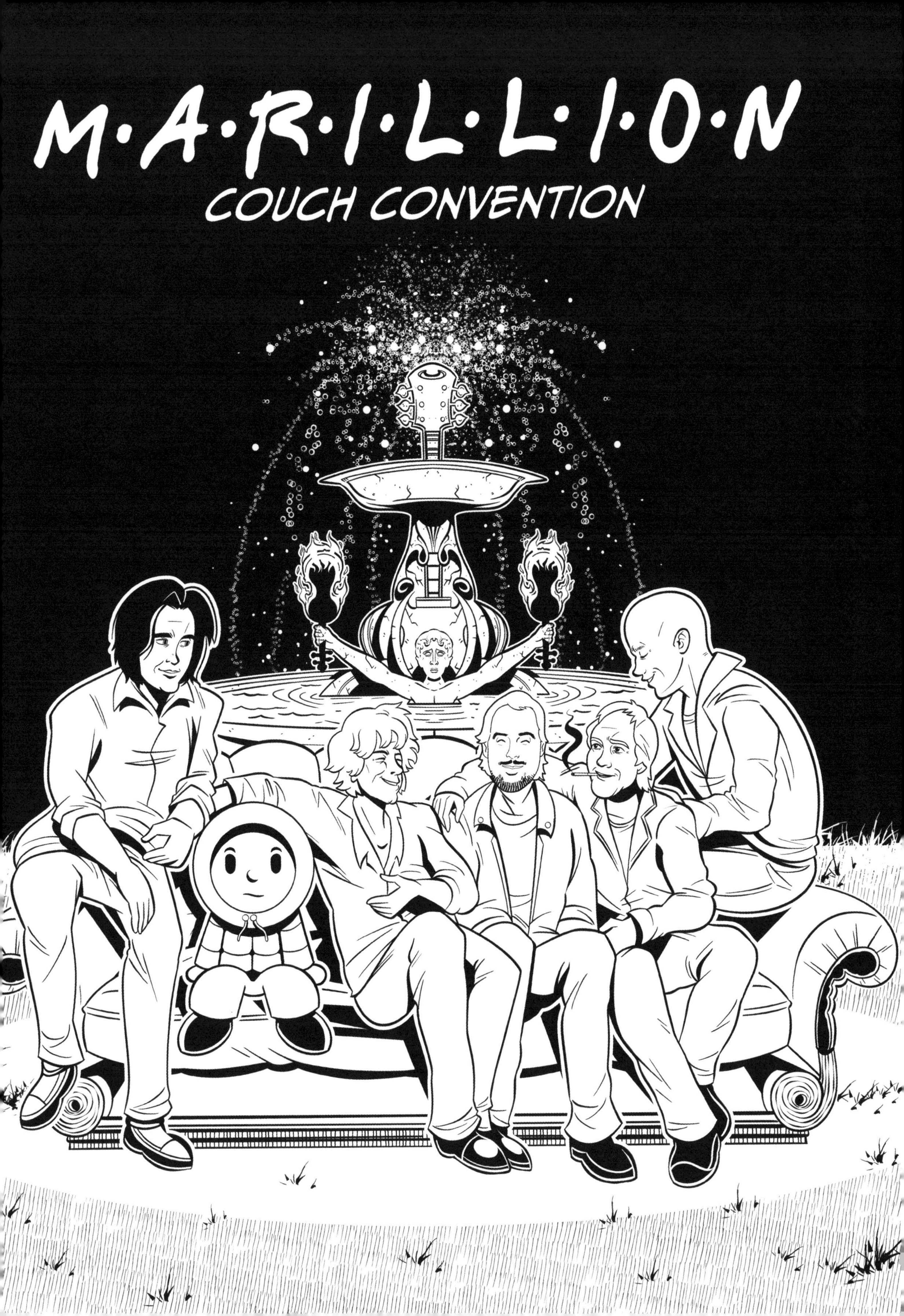
M·A·R·I·L·L·I·O·N
COUCH CONVENTION

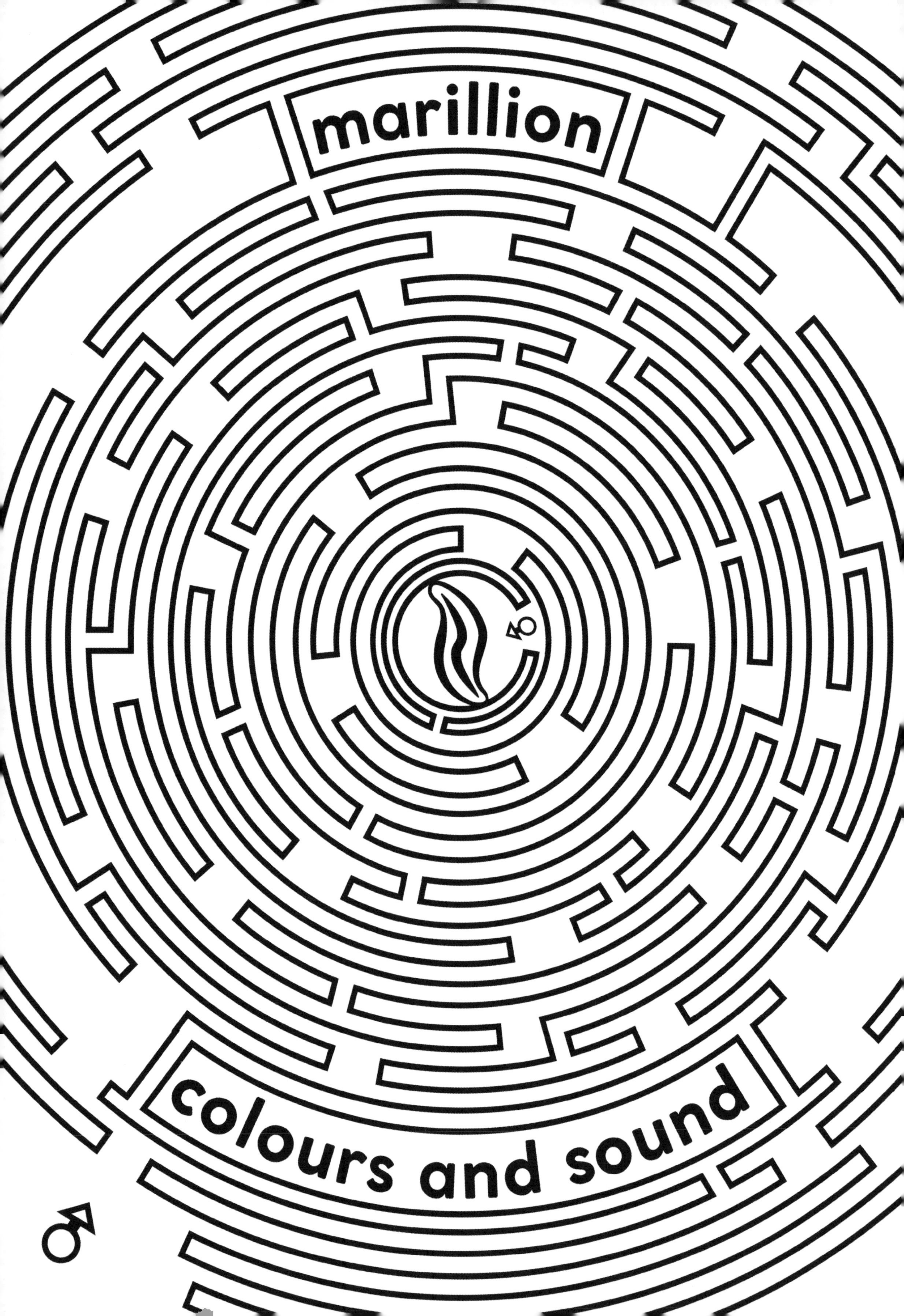
marillion
colours and sound

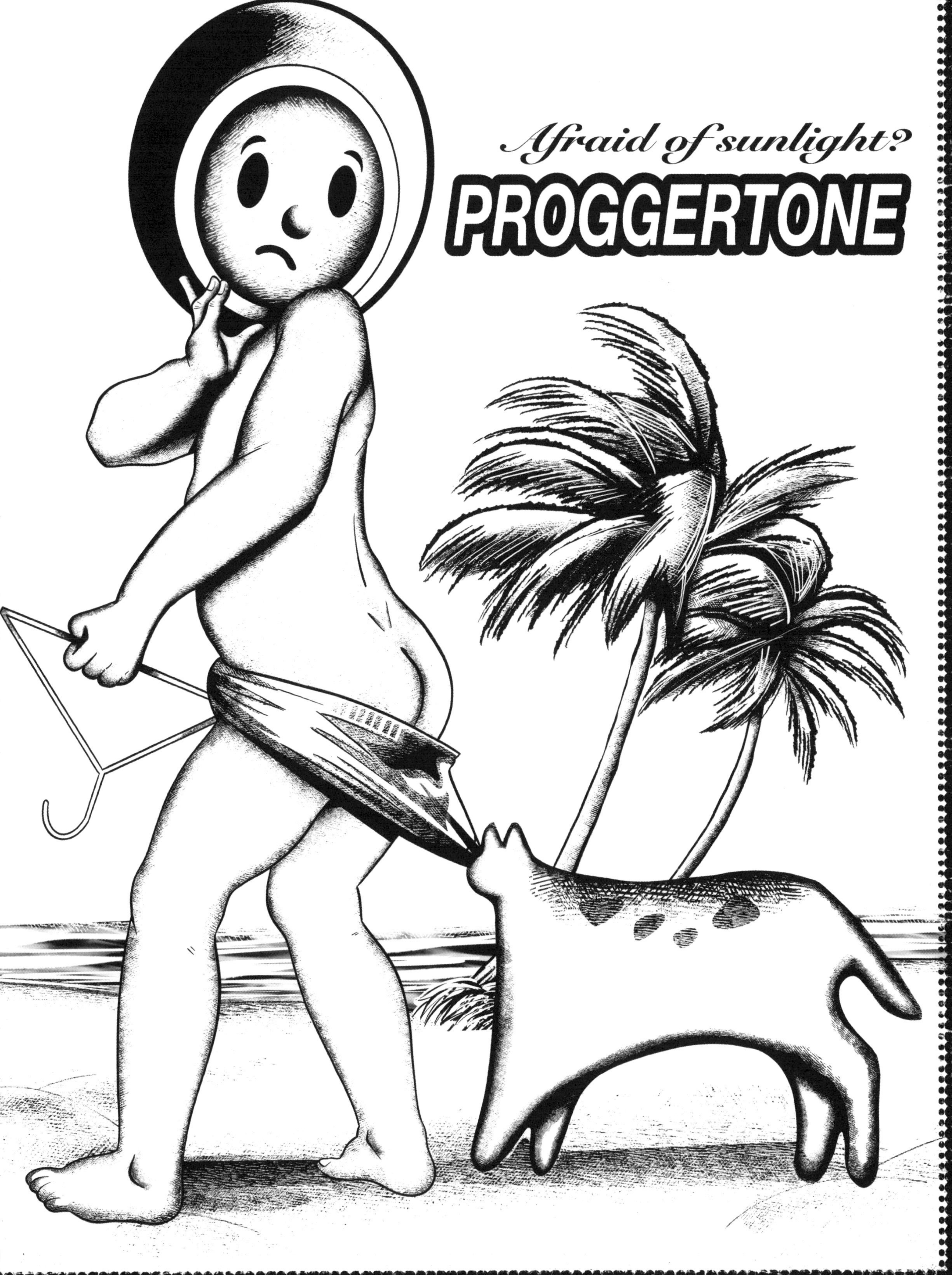

Afraid of sunlight?
PROGGERTONE

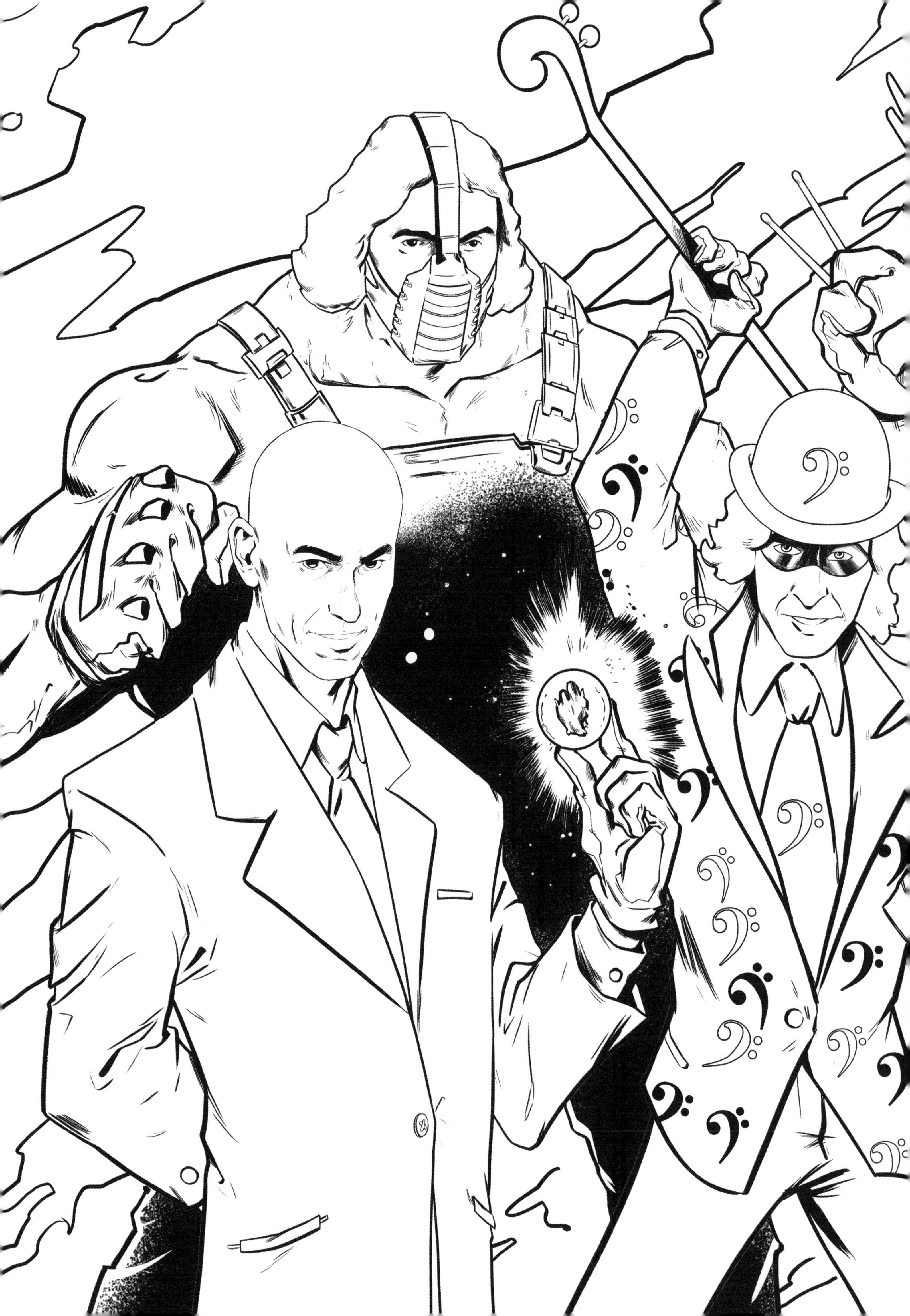

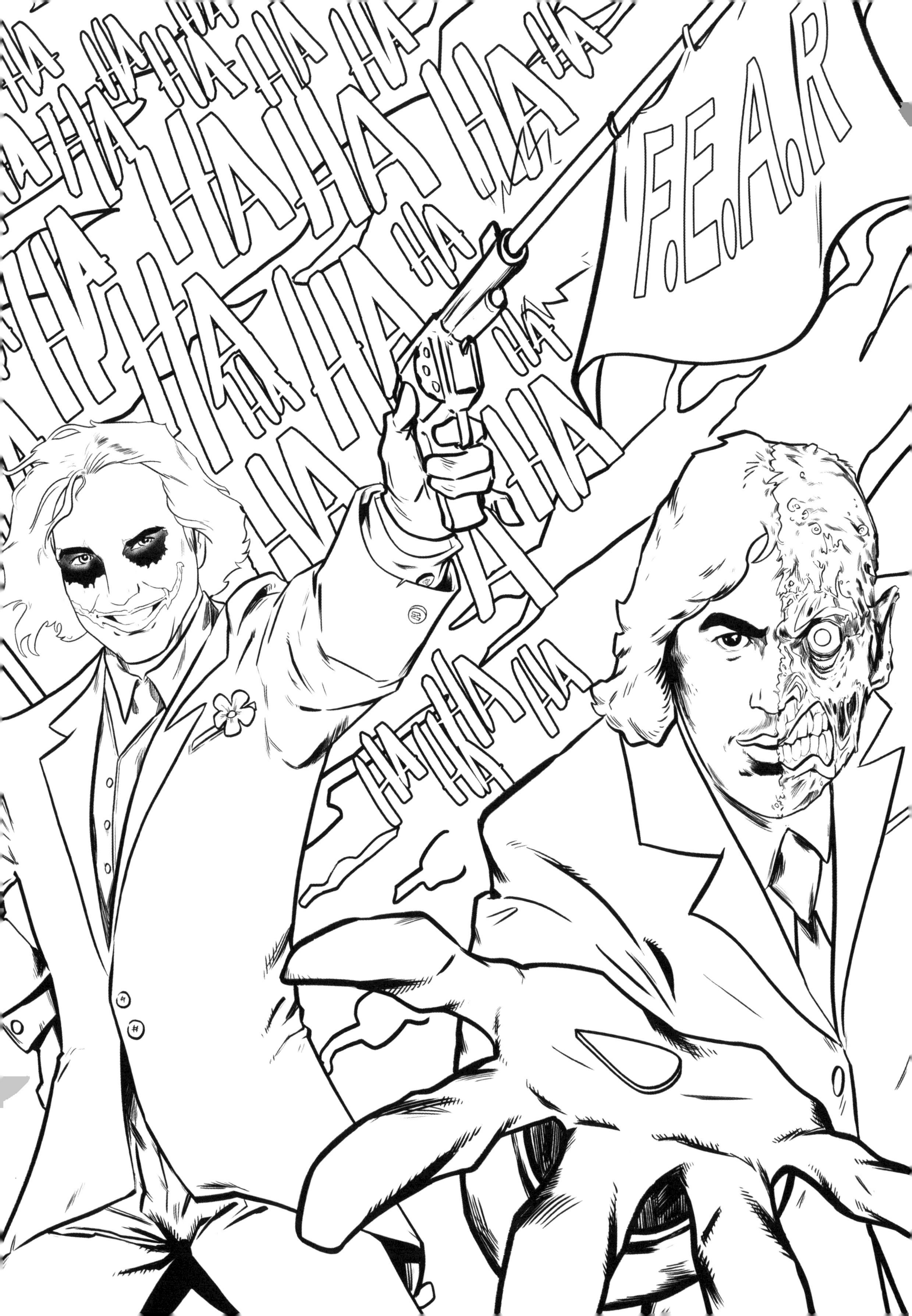
F.E.A.R
HA HA HA HA

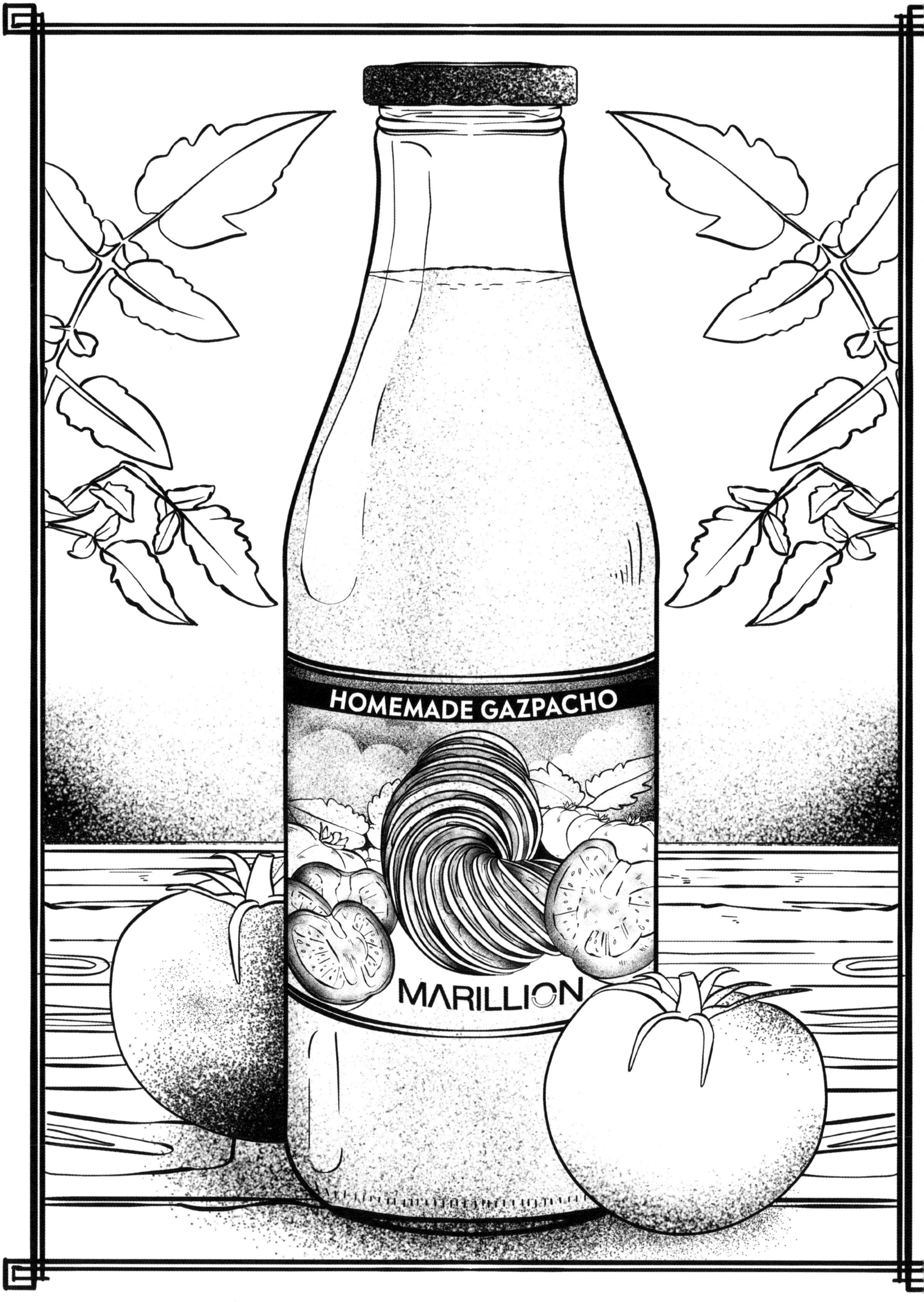
HOMEMADE GAZPACHO
MARILLION

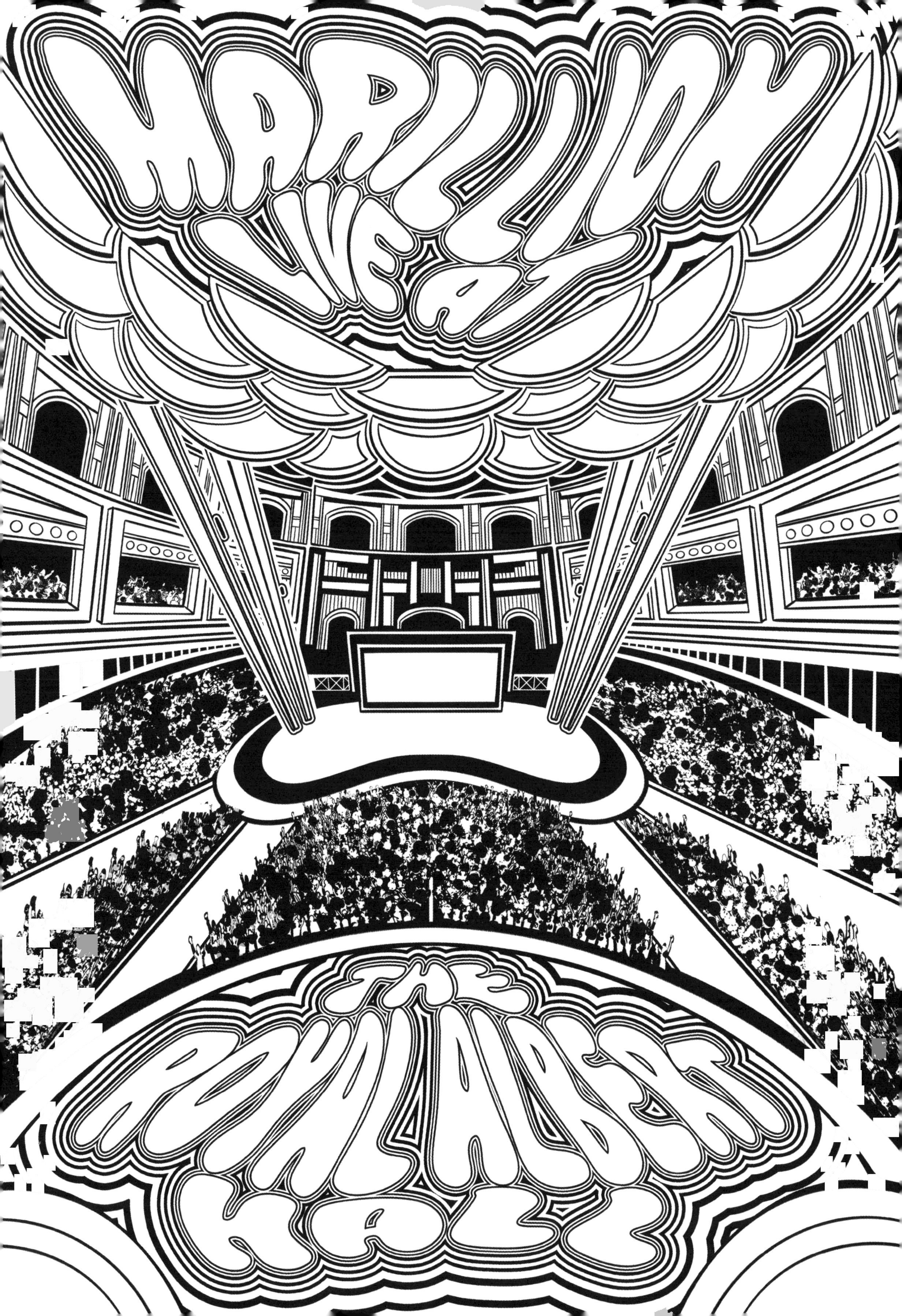
MARILLION
LIVE AT
THE
ROYAL ALBERT
HALL

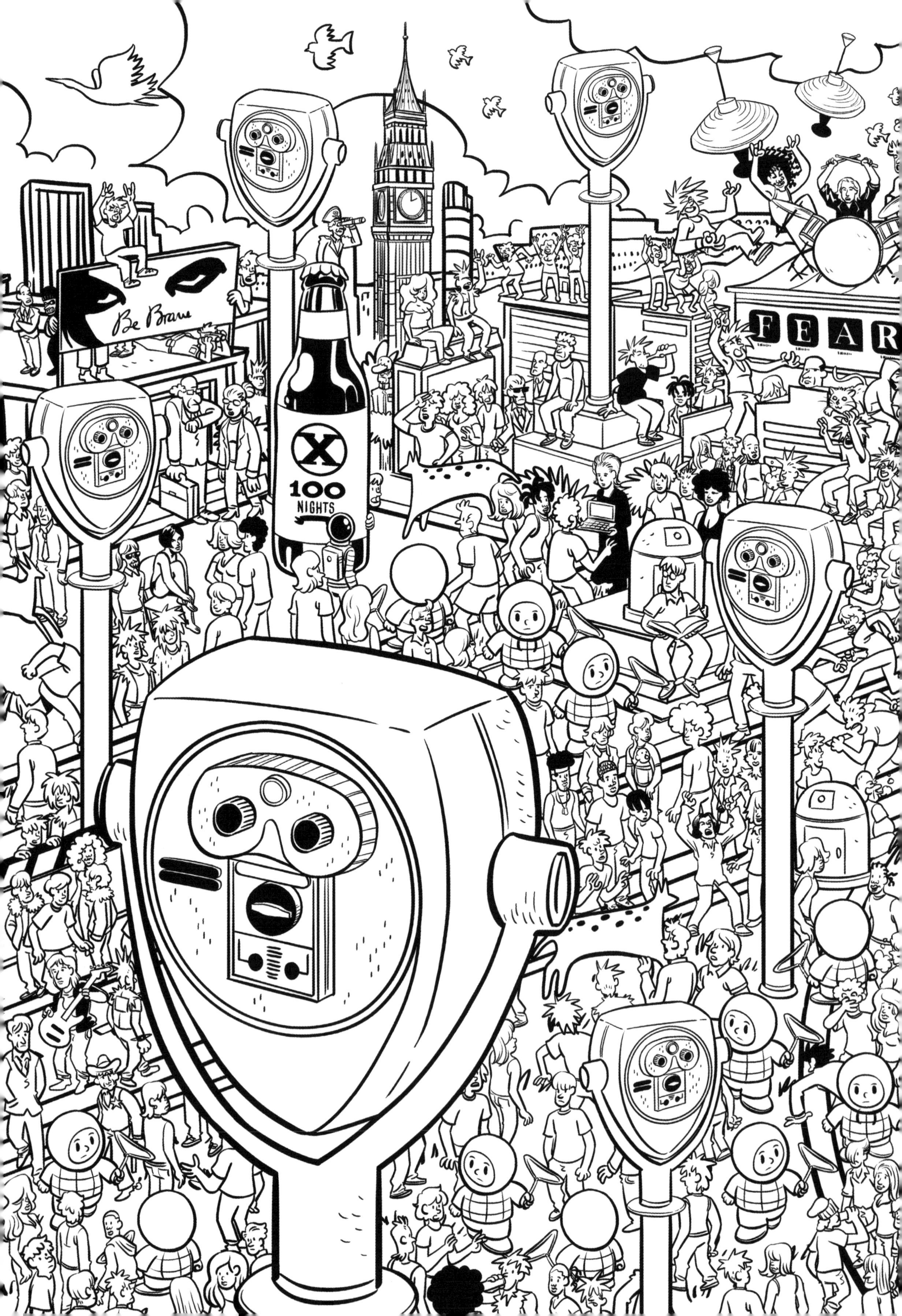
Be Brave
X
100
NIGHTS
FEAR

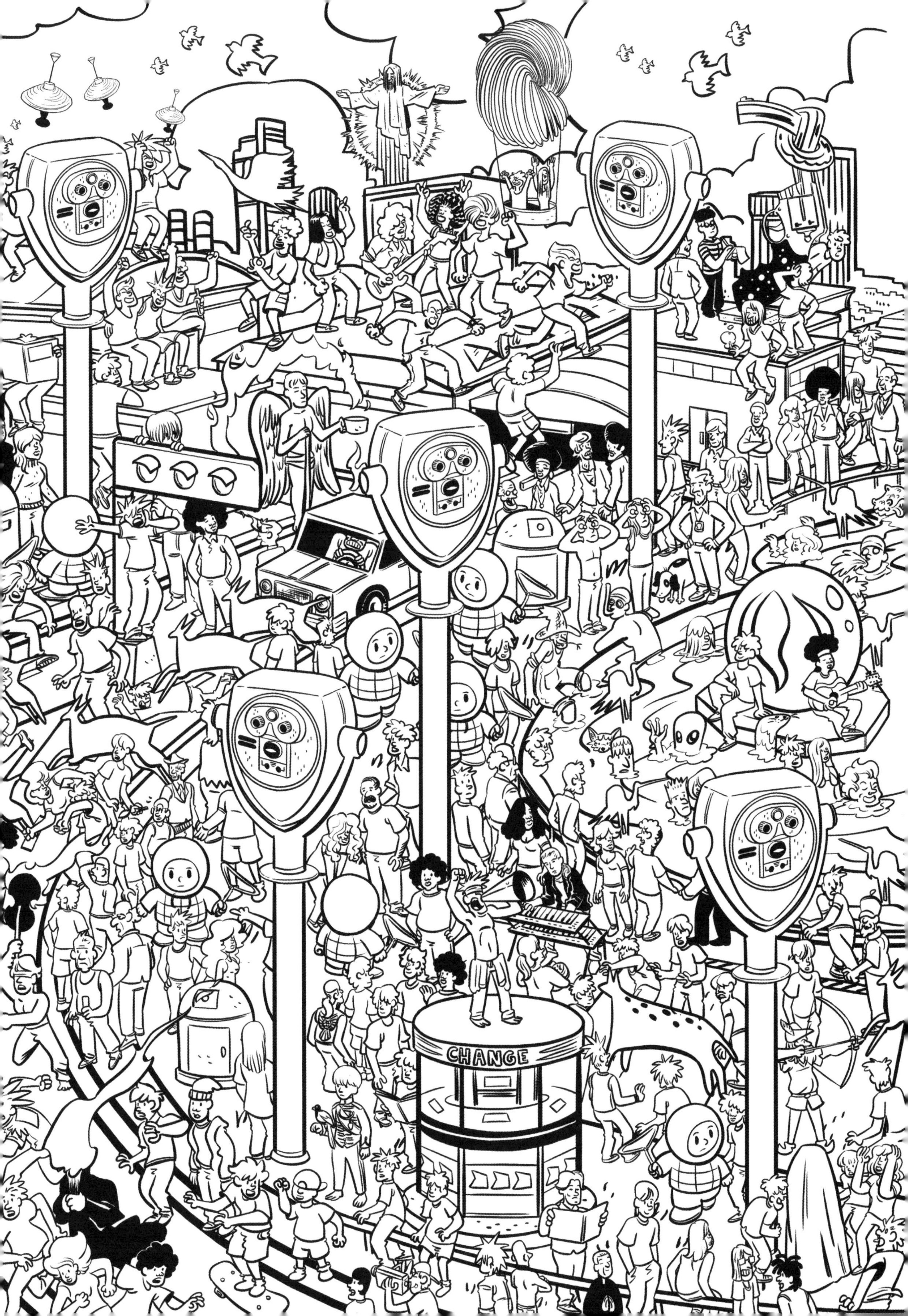
CHANGE

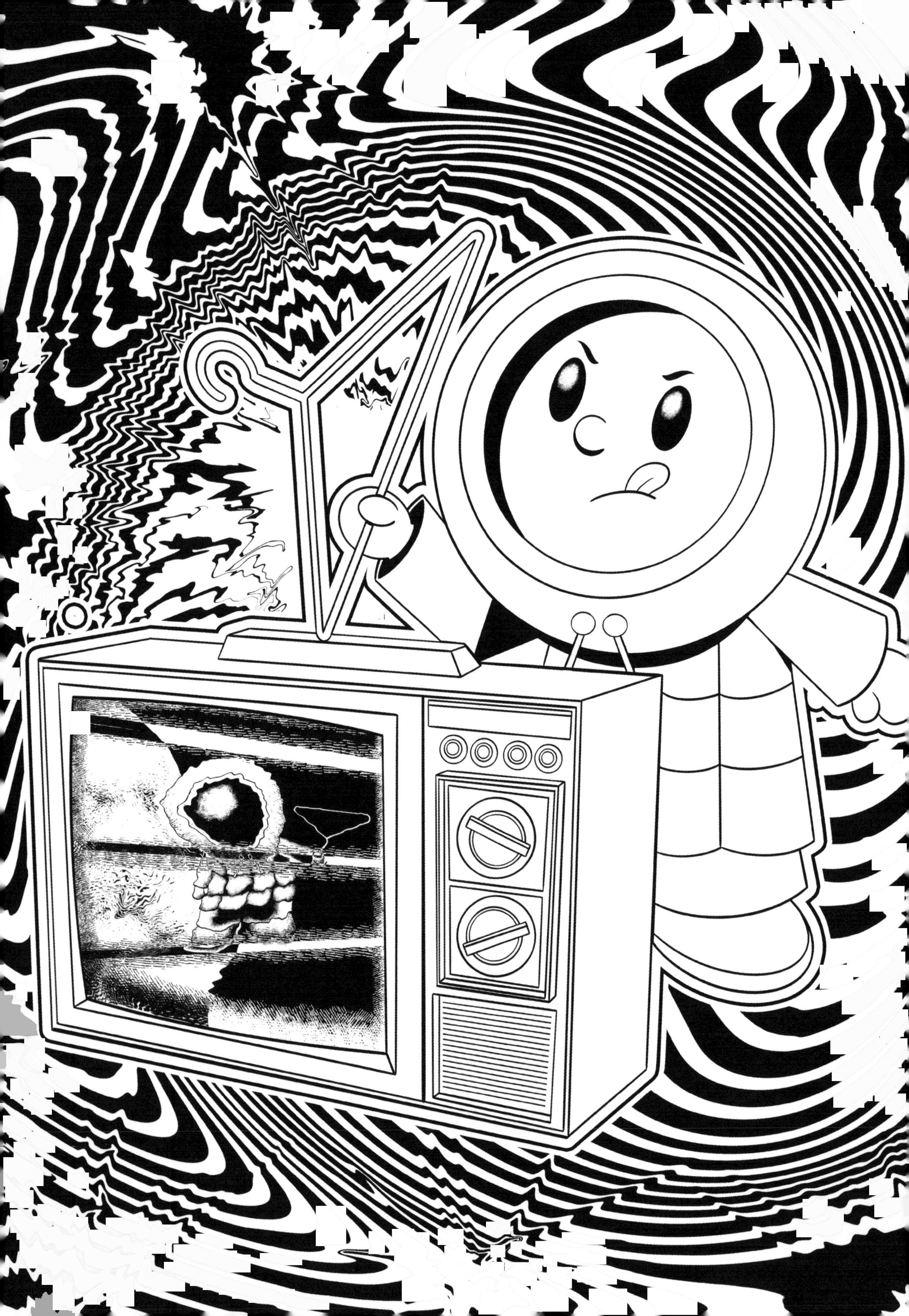

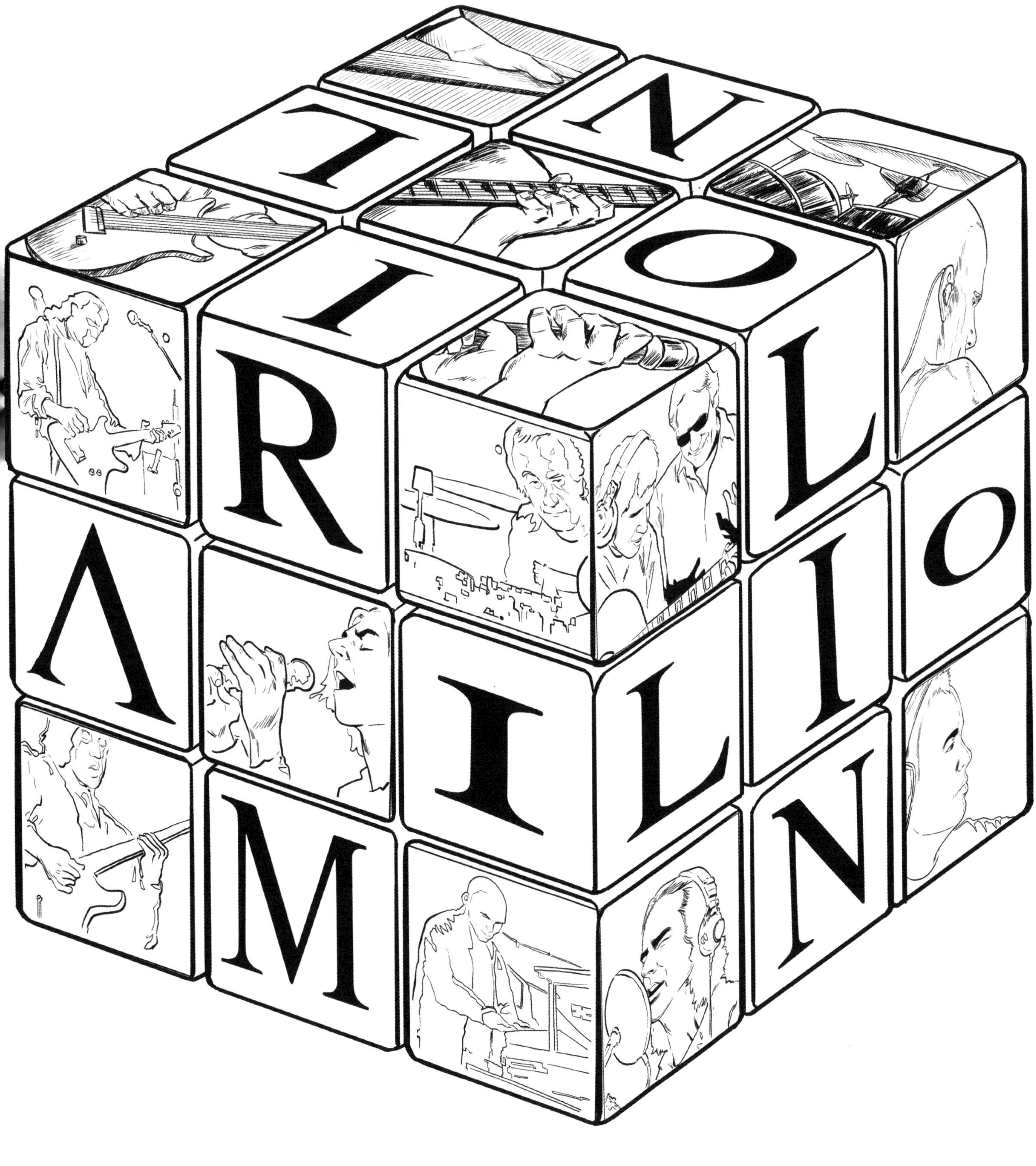

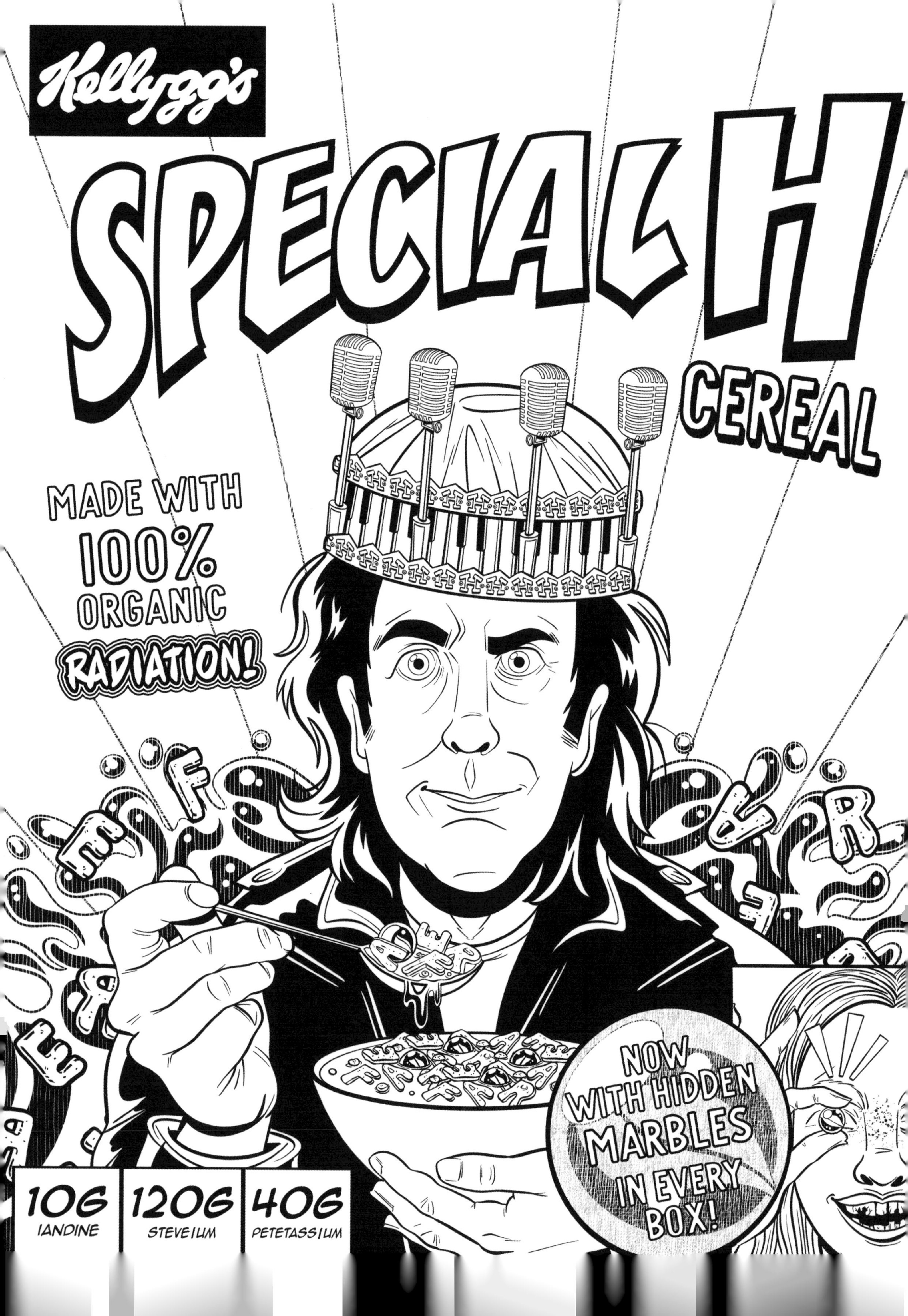
Kellygg's
SPECIAL H
CEREAL
MADE WITH 100% ORGANIC RADIATION!
NOW WITH HIDDEN MARBLES IN EVERY BOX!
10G IANDINE
120G STEVEIUM
40G PETETASSIUM

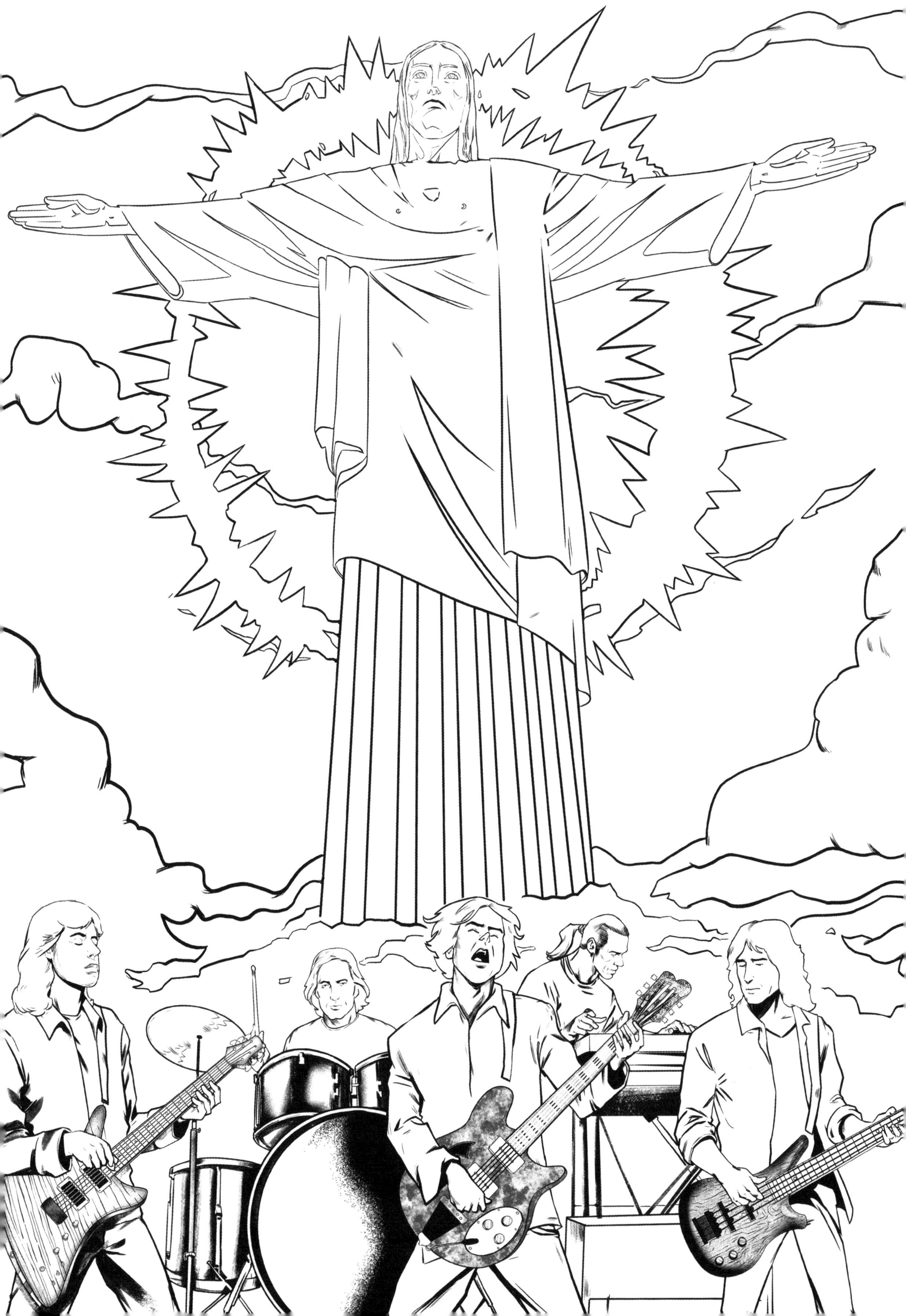

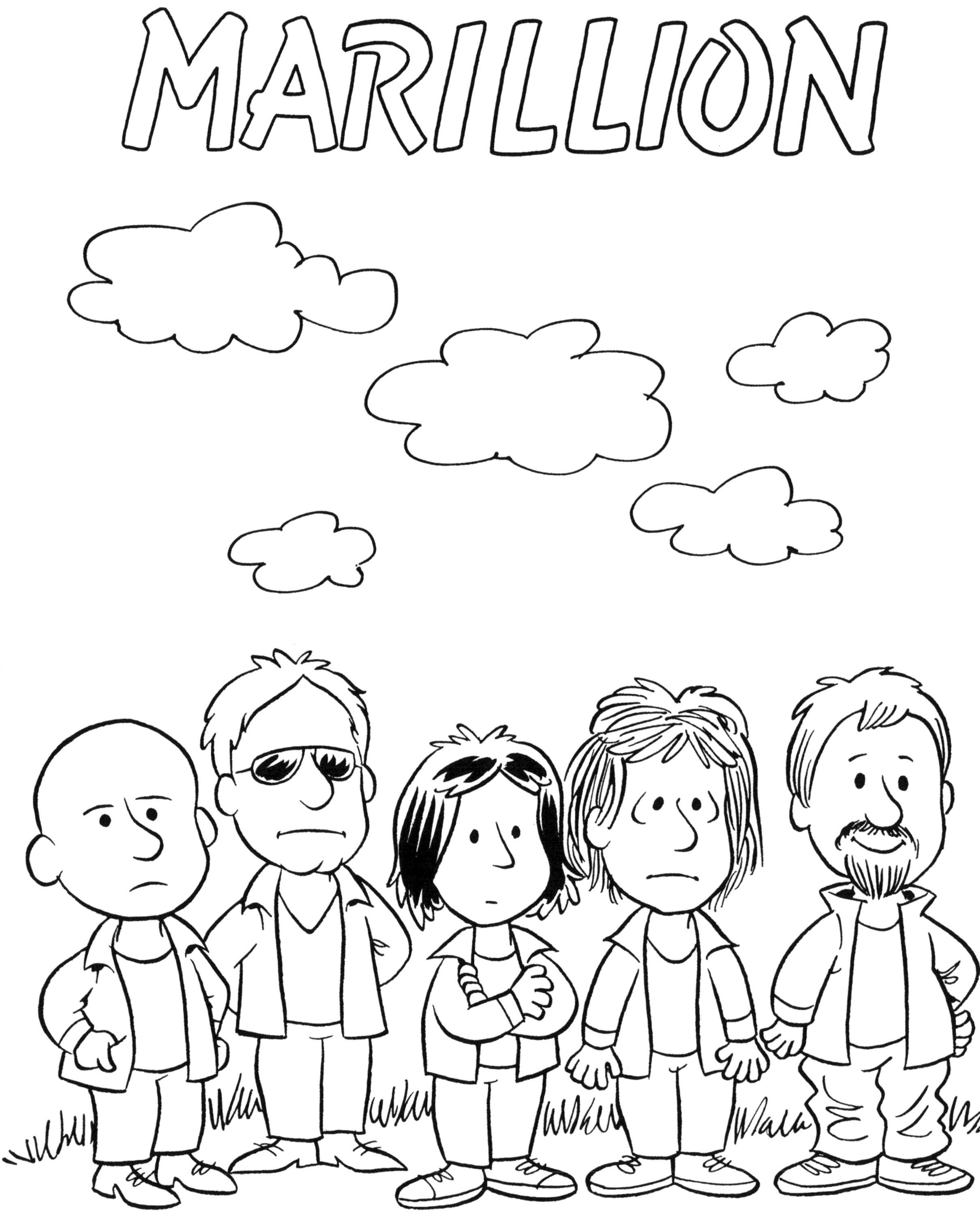
MARILLION

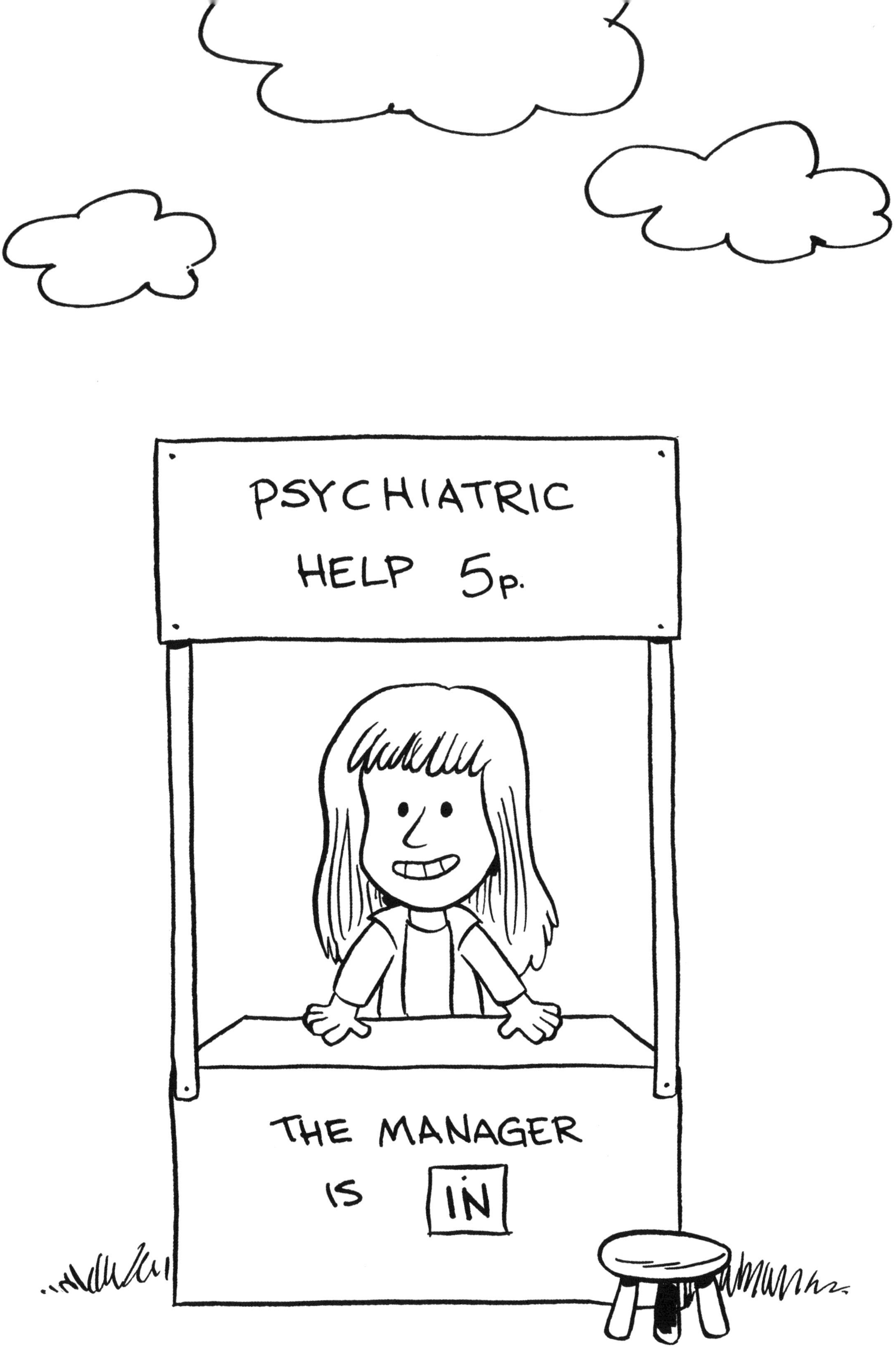
PSYCHIATRIC
HELP 5p.
THE MANAGER
IS IN

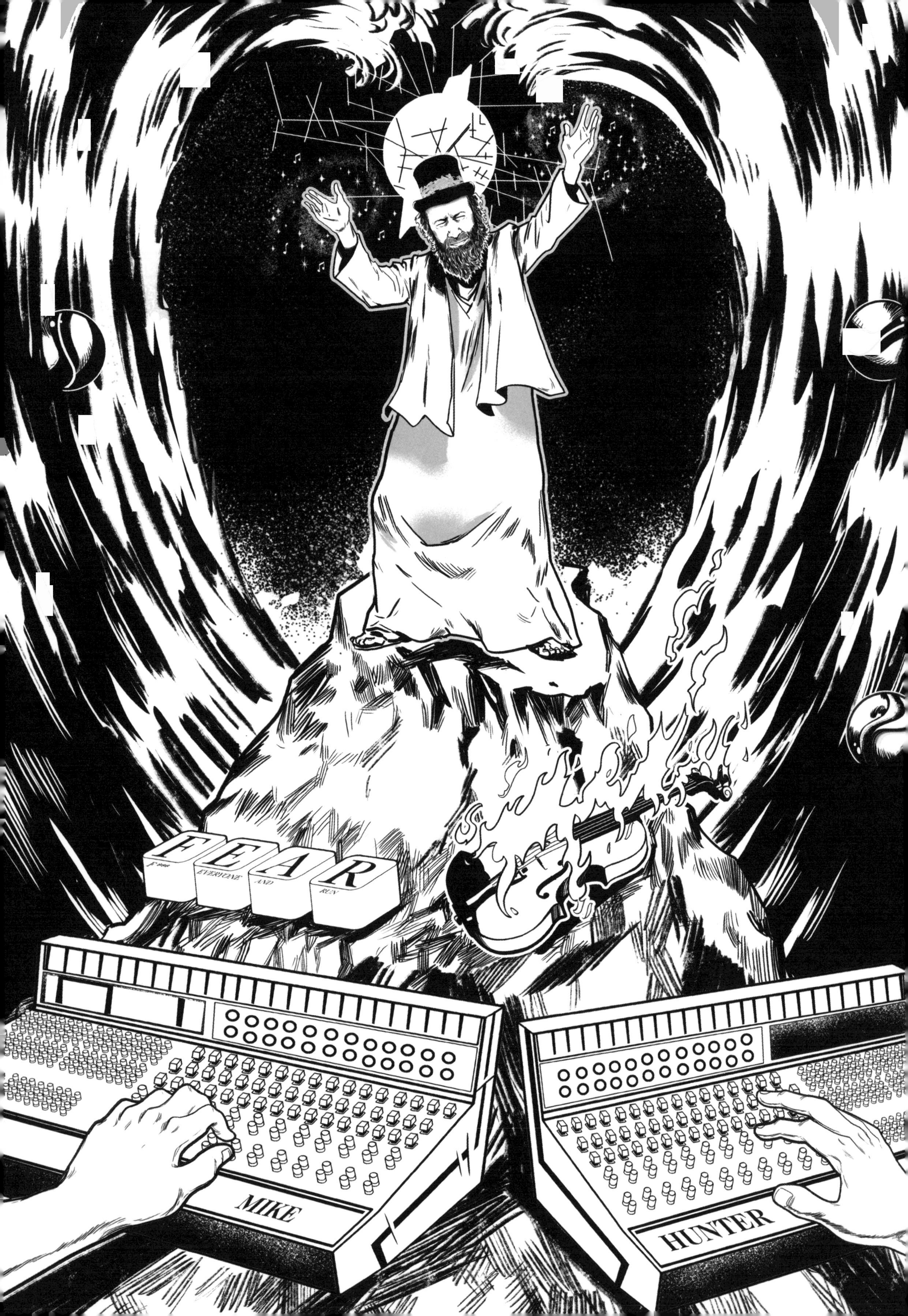
FEAR
EVERYONE
AND
RUN
MIKE
HUNTER

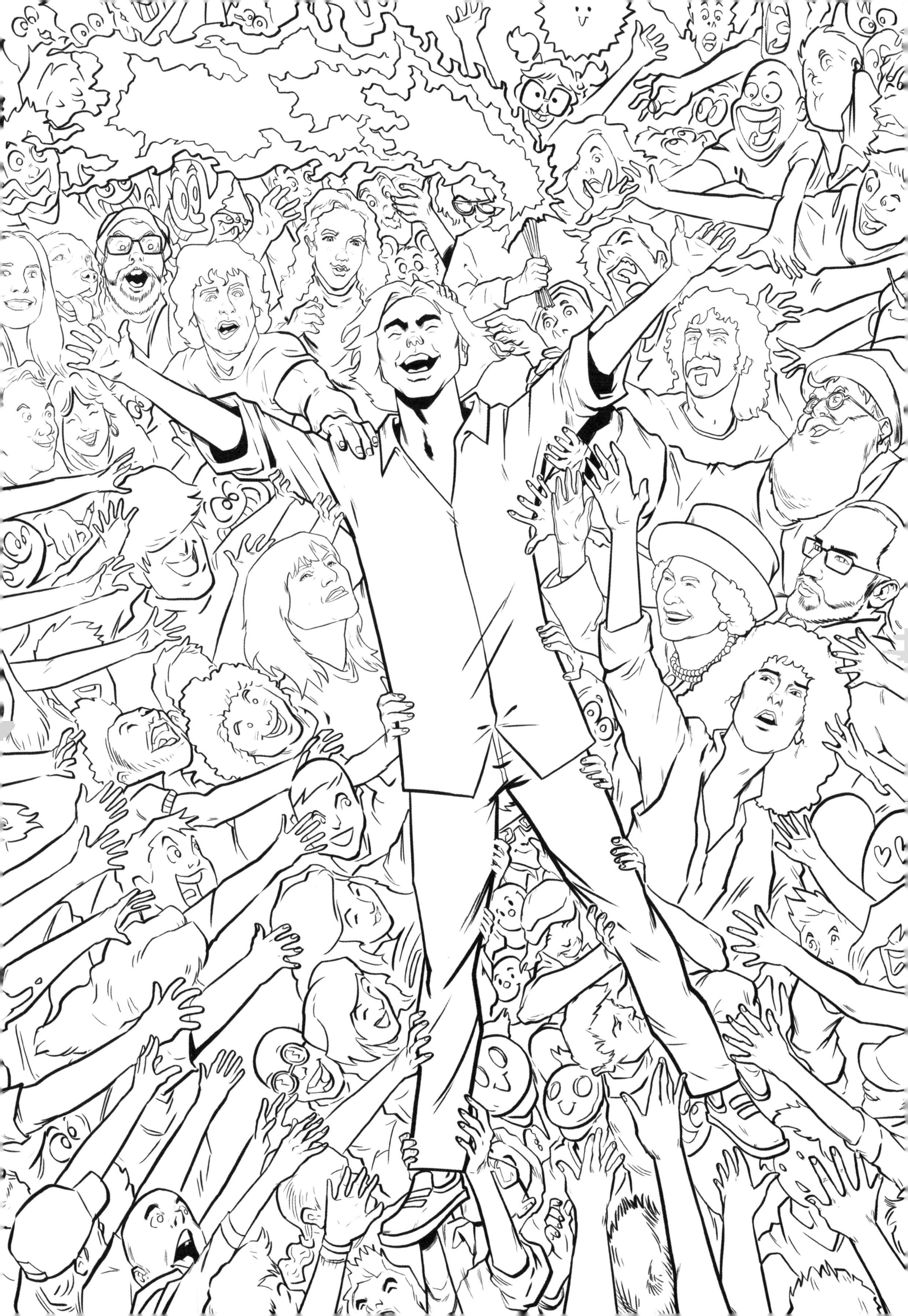

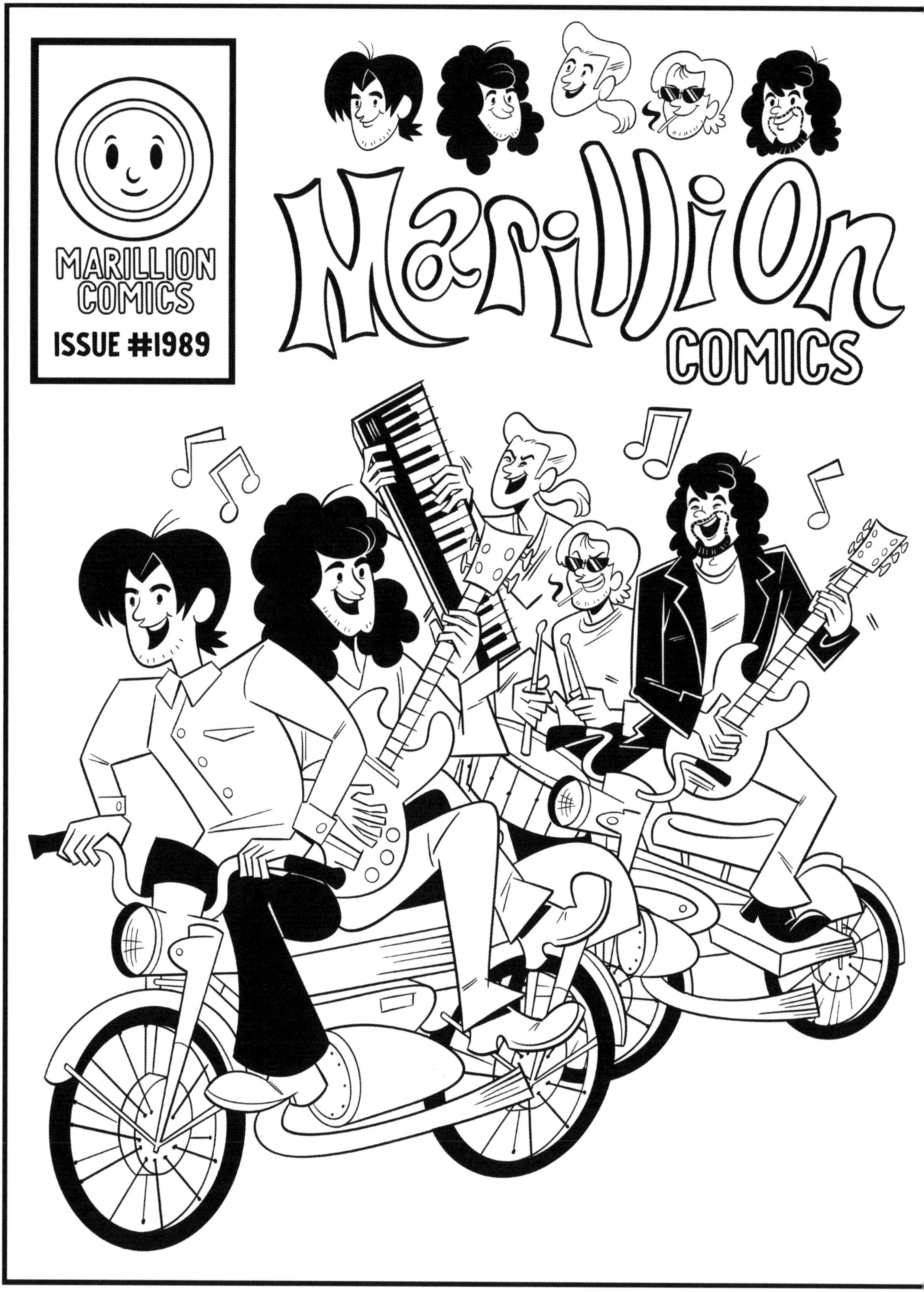
MARILLION COMICS
ISSUE #1989
Marillion
COMICS

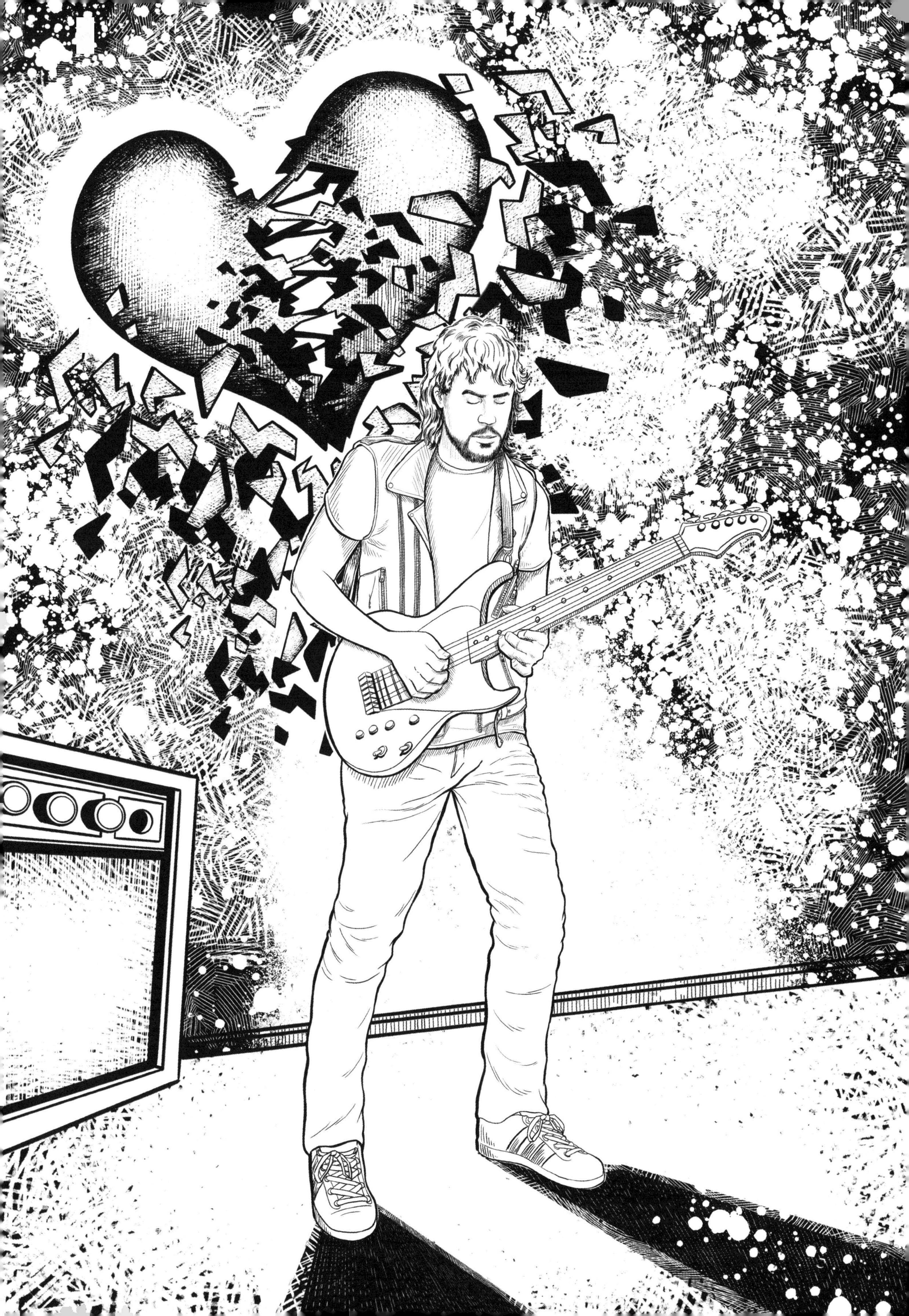

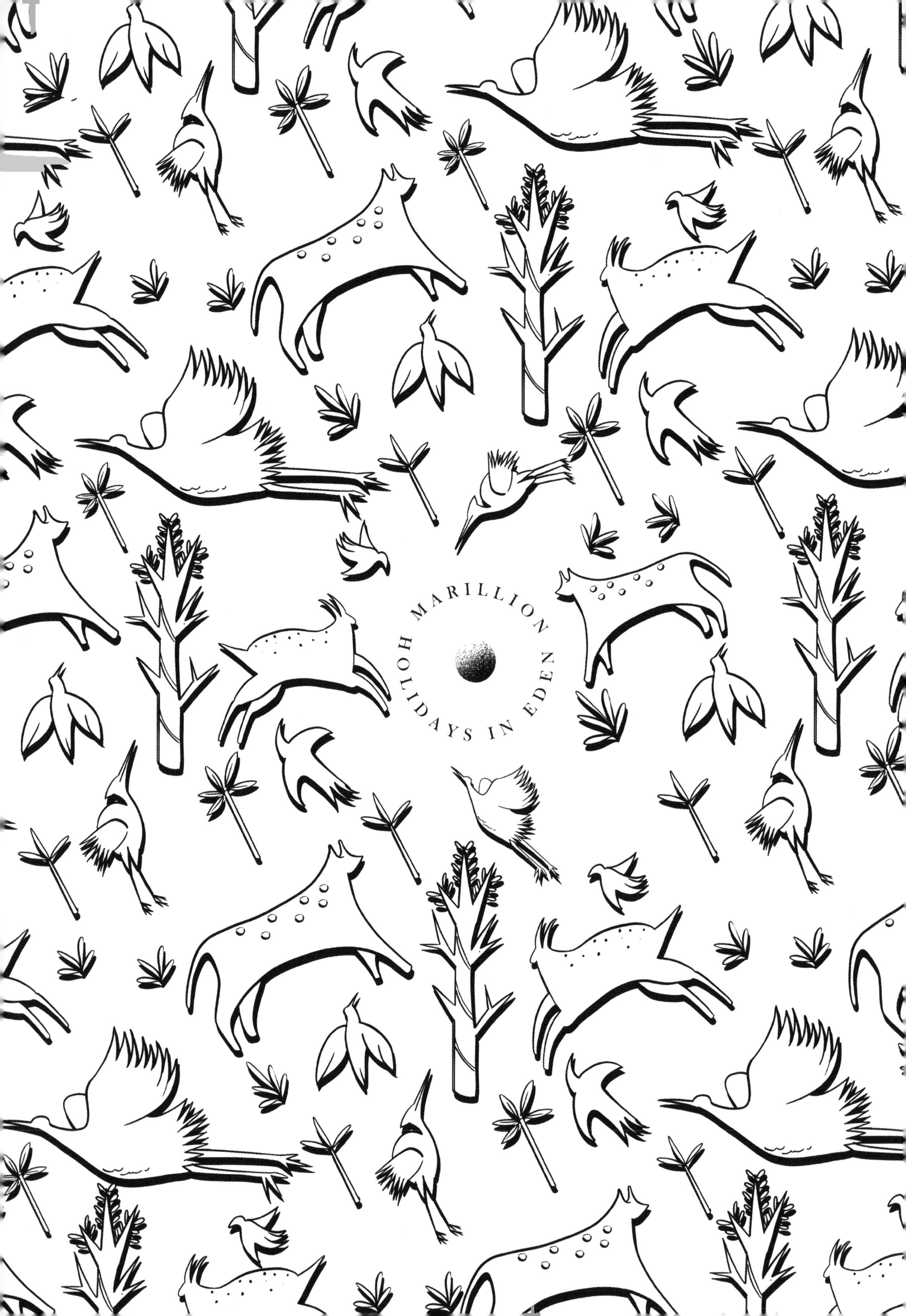
MARILLION
HOLIDAYS IN EDEN

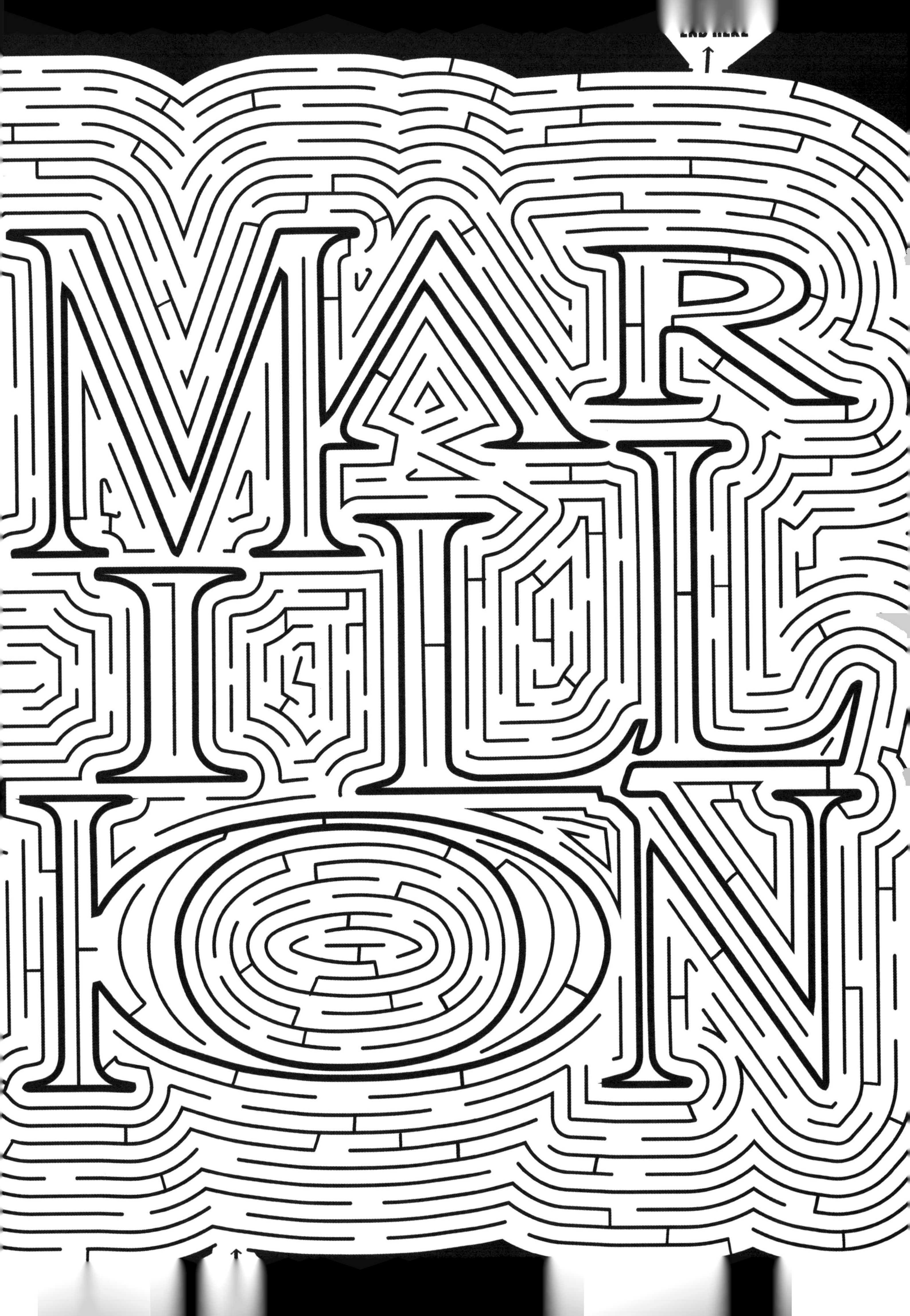

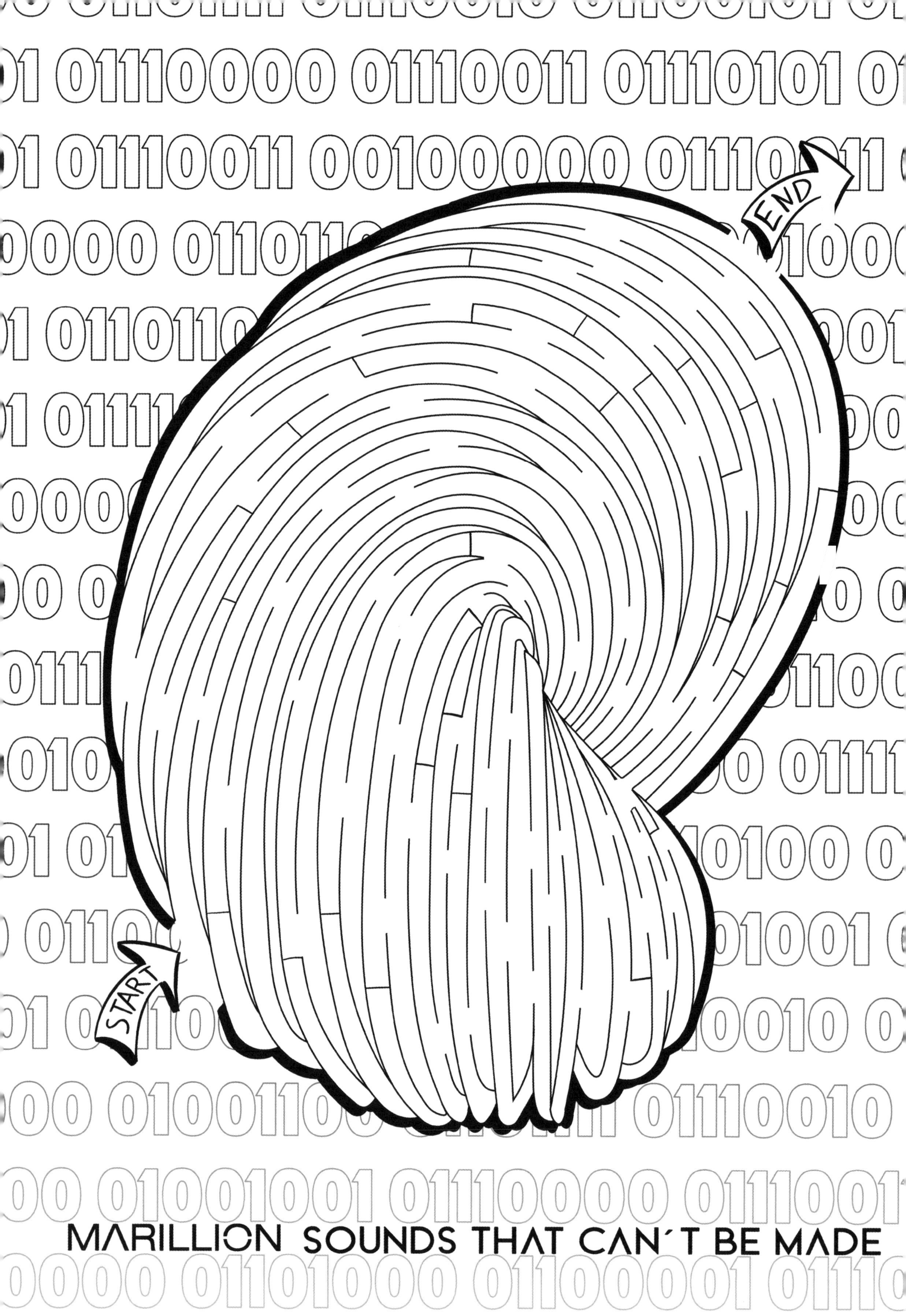
START
END
MARILLION SOUNDS THAT CAN´T BE MADE

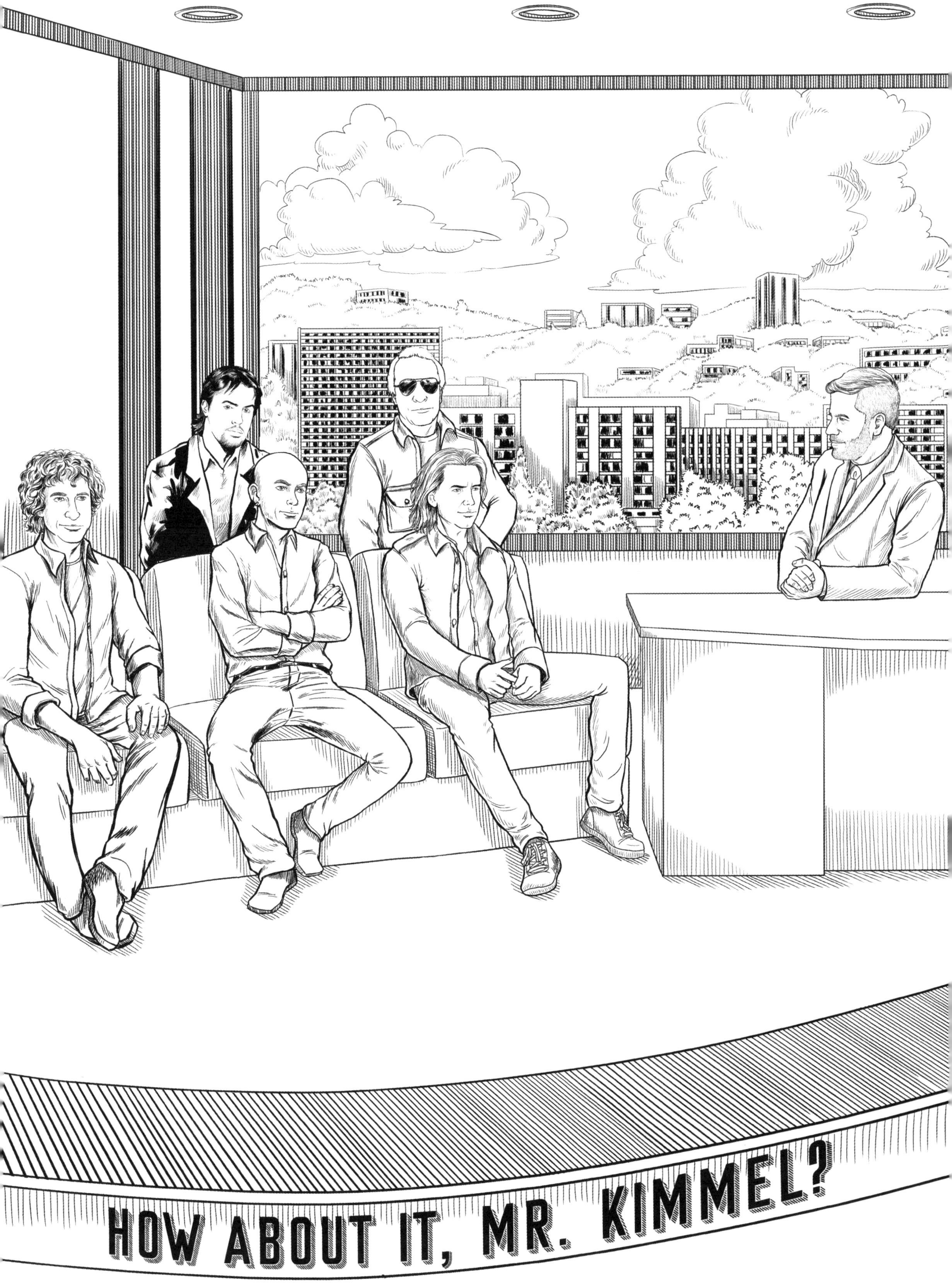
HOW ABOUT IT, MR. KIMMEL?

Ho

Ed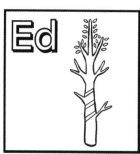

No

Br

Gr

Af

Af²

Be

En

Ch

Ra

Po

Cm

Ak^UK

Aw

El

Fa

In

Jn

Mr

Ra

Sm

Pu

Fe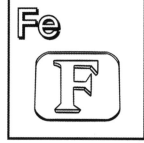

Bb

Sz

Sw

Sw^Ln

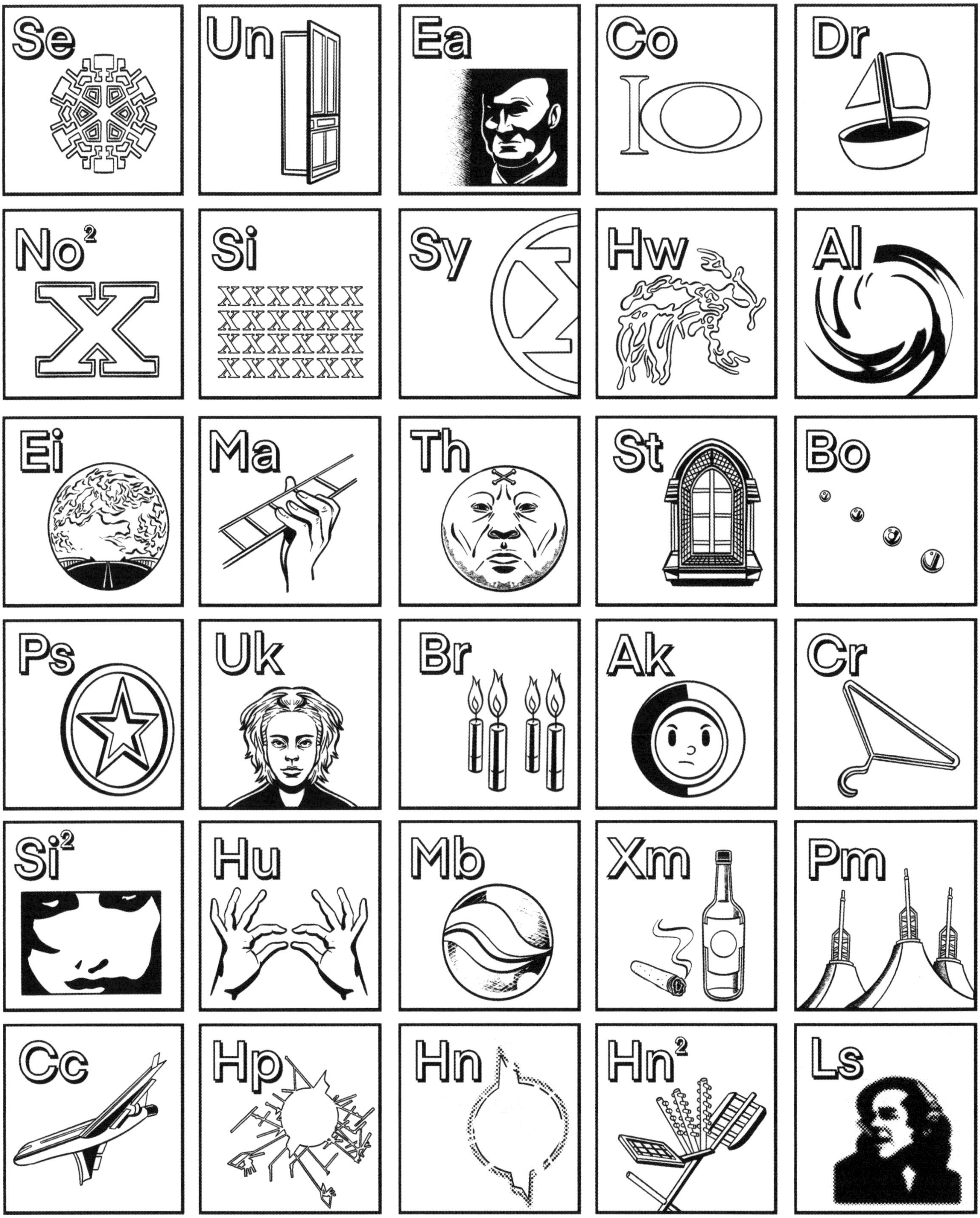
Se
Un
Ea
Co
Dr
No^2
Si
Sy
Hw
Al
Ei
Ma
Th
St
Bo
Ps
Uk
Br
Ak
Cr
Si^2
Hu
Mb
Xm
Pm
Cc
Hp
Hn
Hn^2
Ls

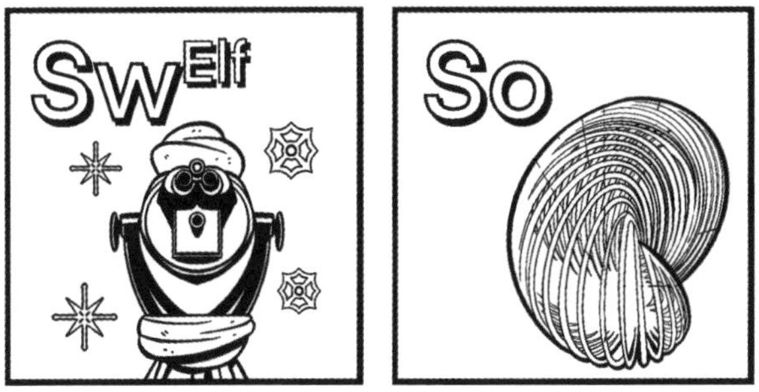
Sw^{Elf}
So

PERIODIC TABLE

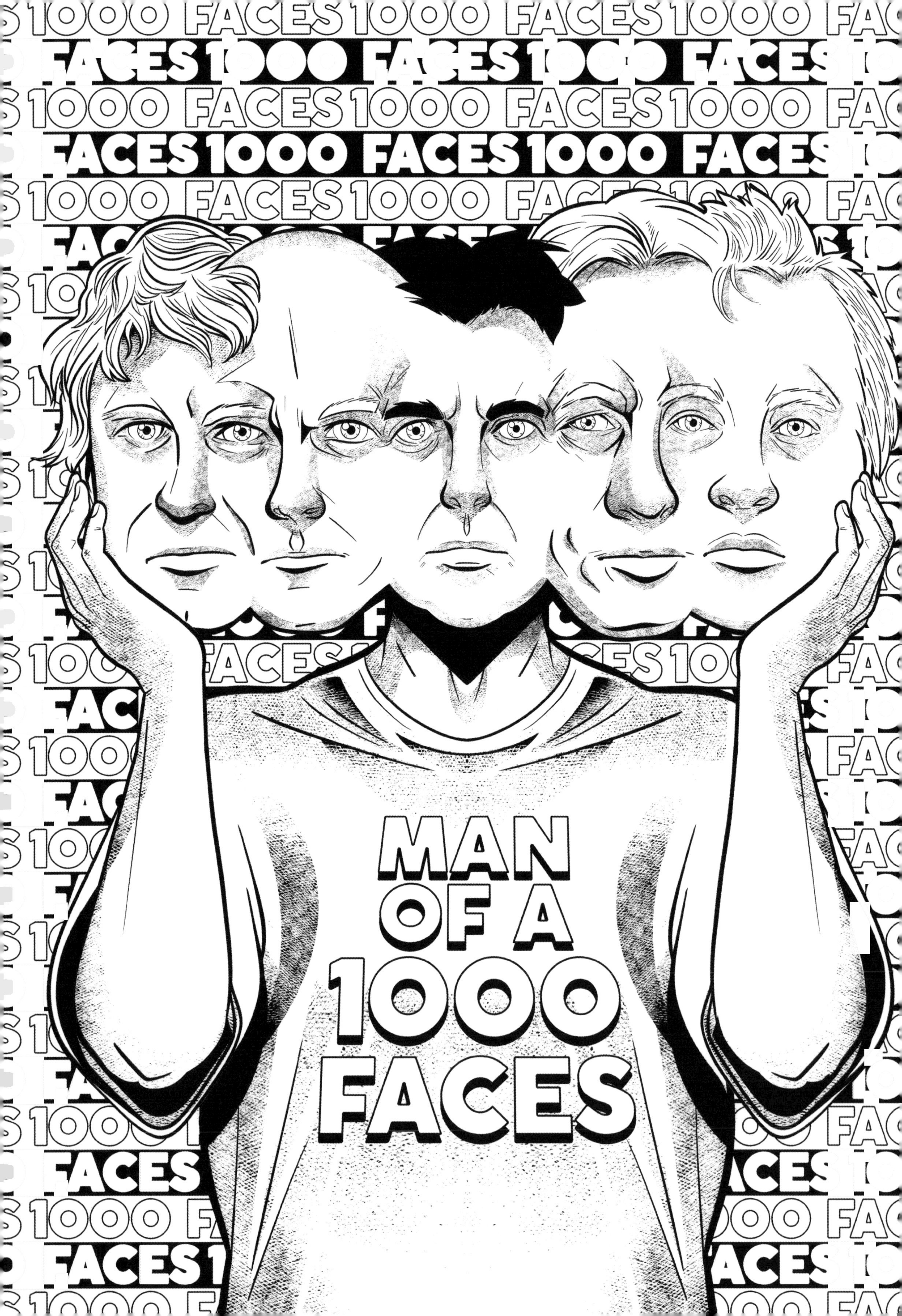
1000 FACES
MAN OF A 1000 FACES

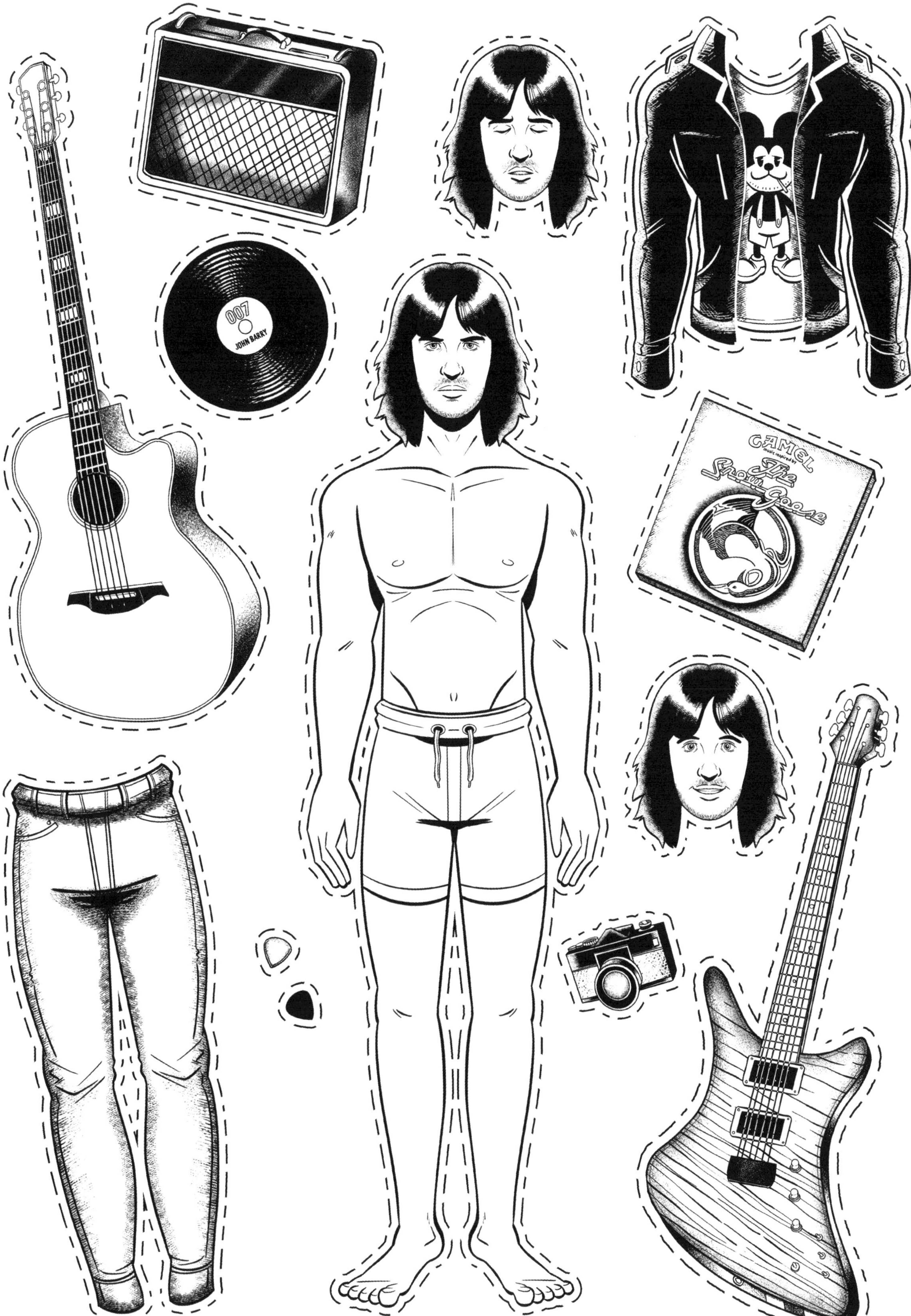
007
JOHN BARRY
CAMEL
music inspired by
The Snow Goose

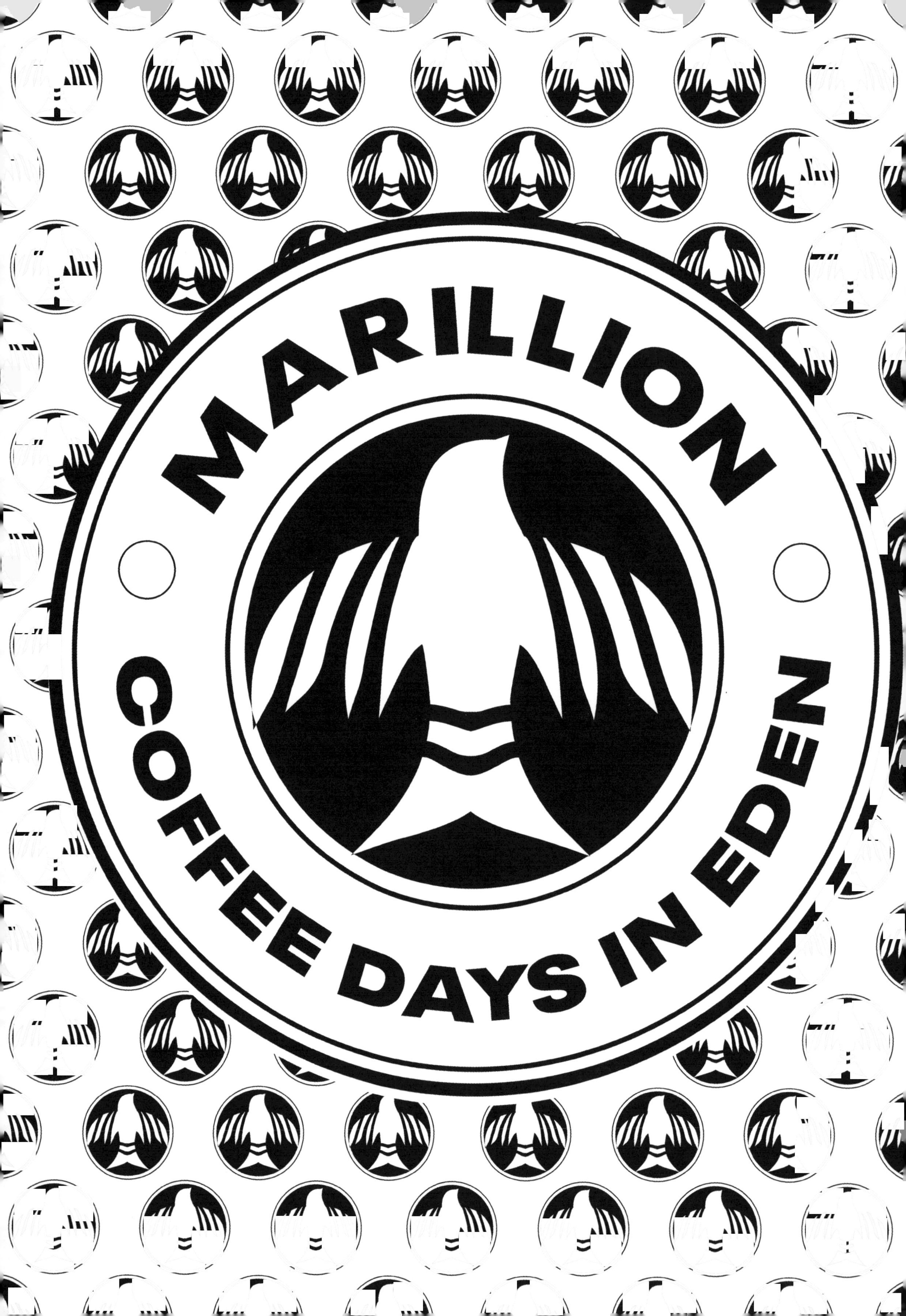
MARILLION
COFFEE DAYS IN EDEN

WAITING TO HAPPEN

MARILLION COFFEE

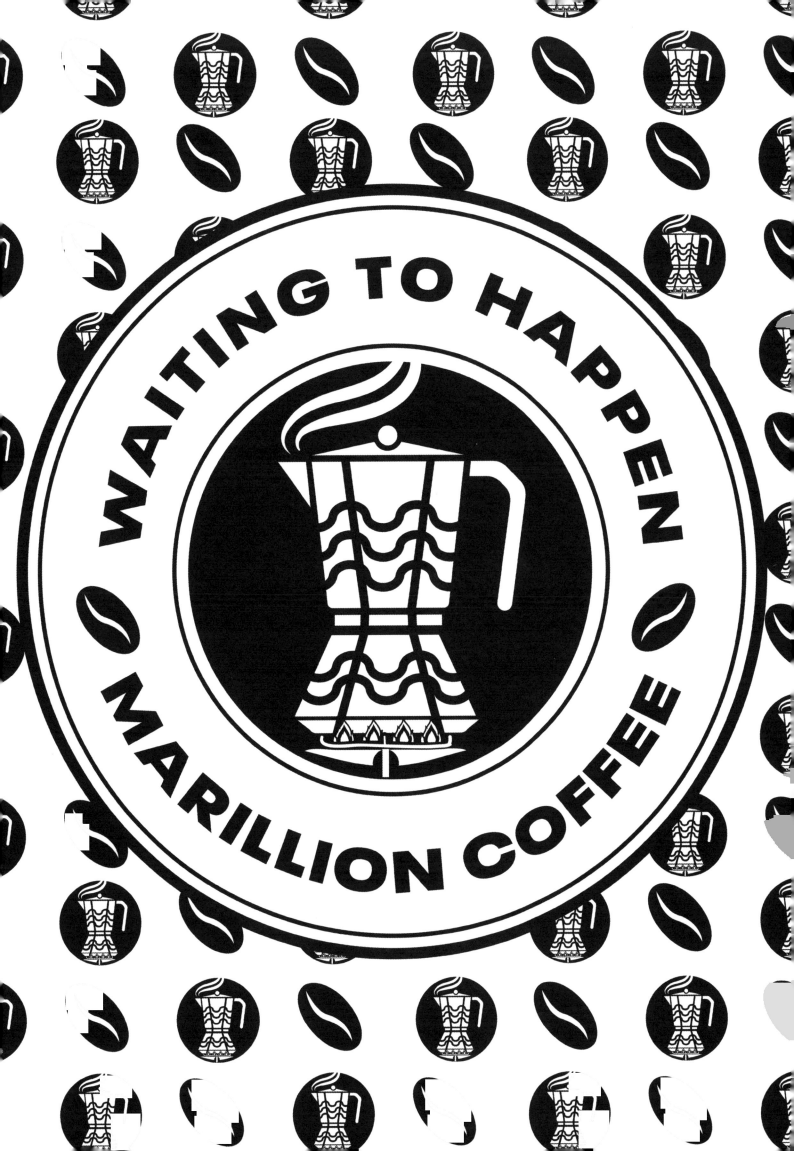

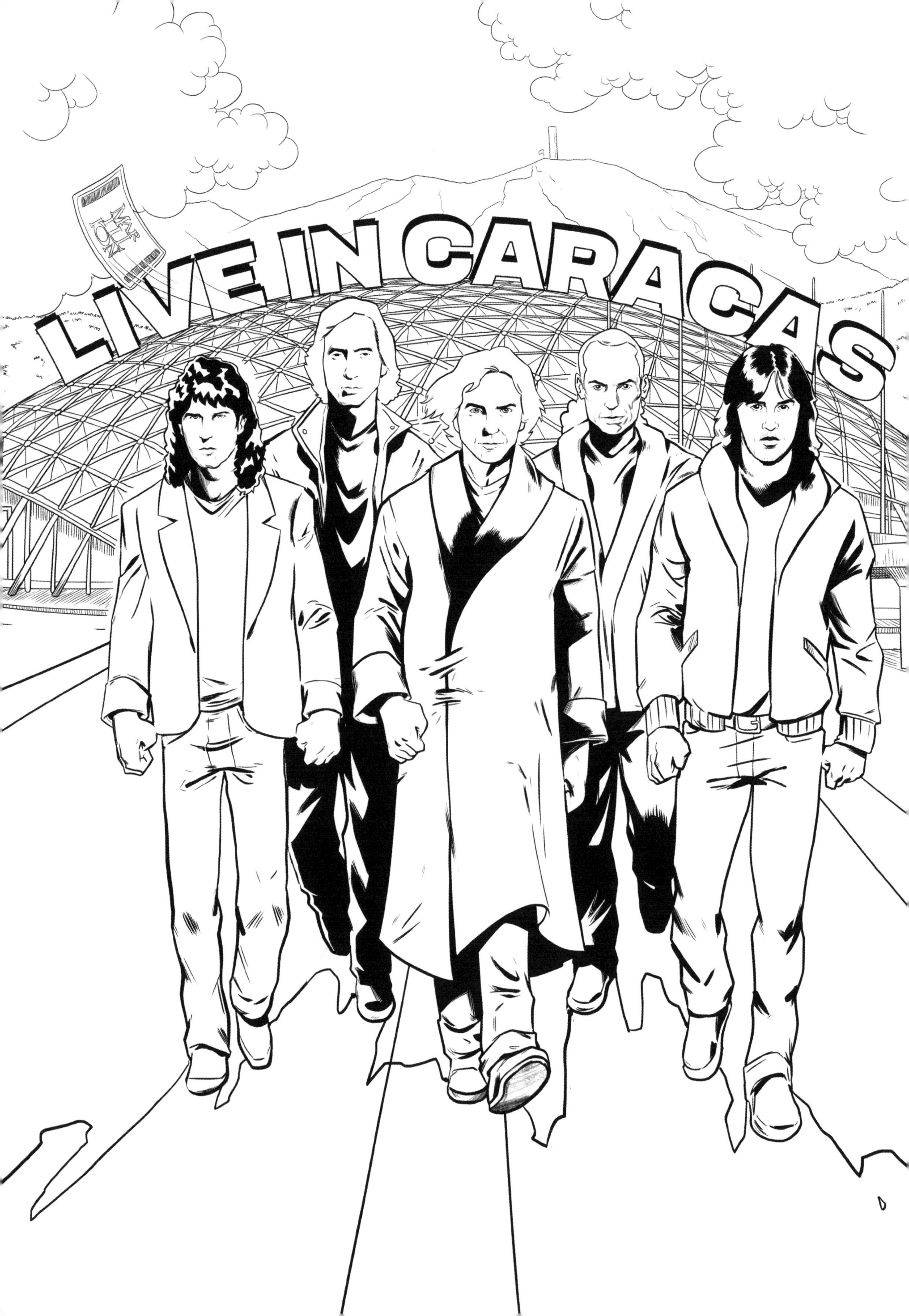
LIVE IN CARACAS

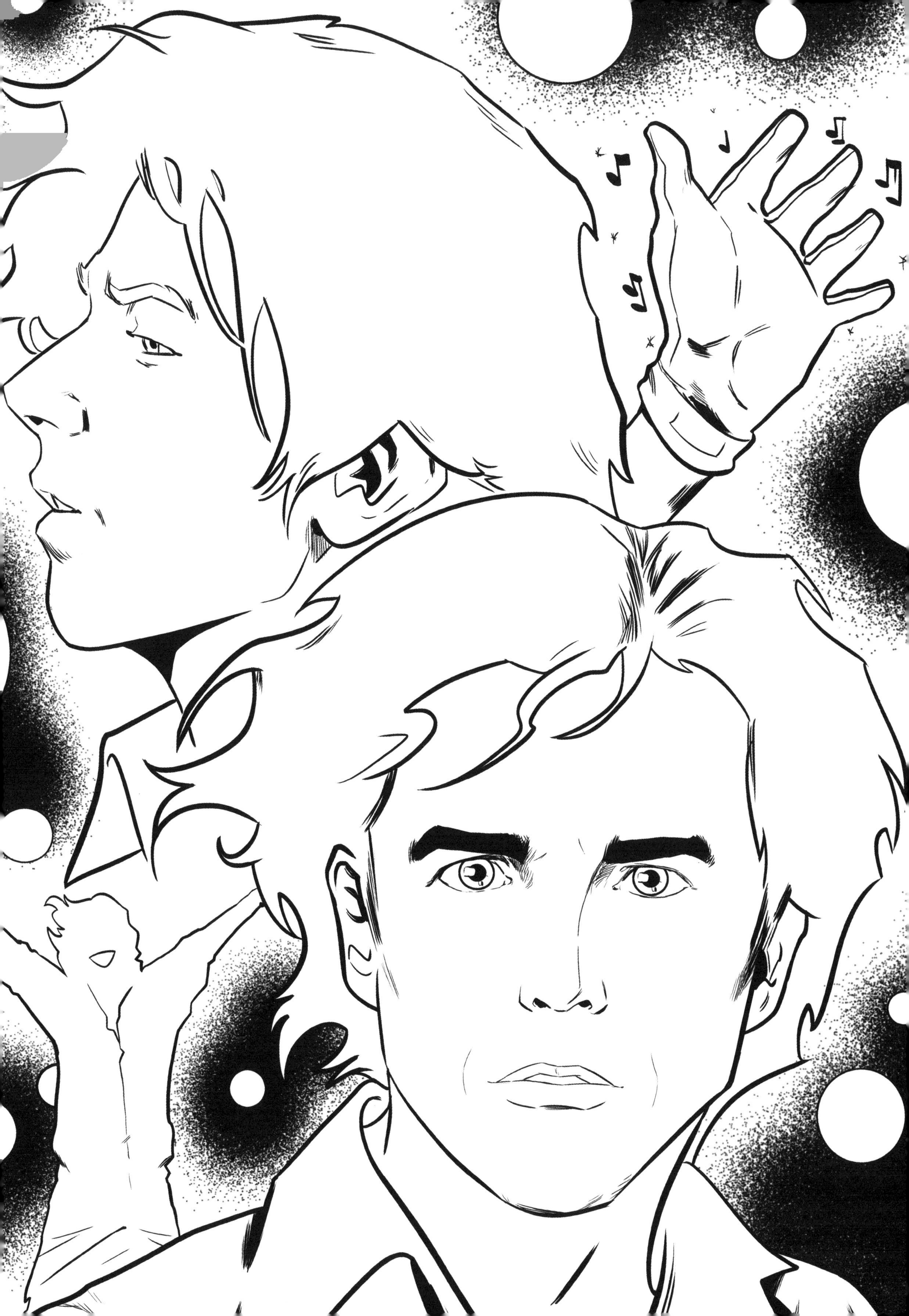

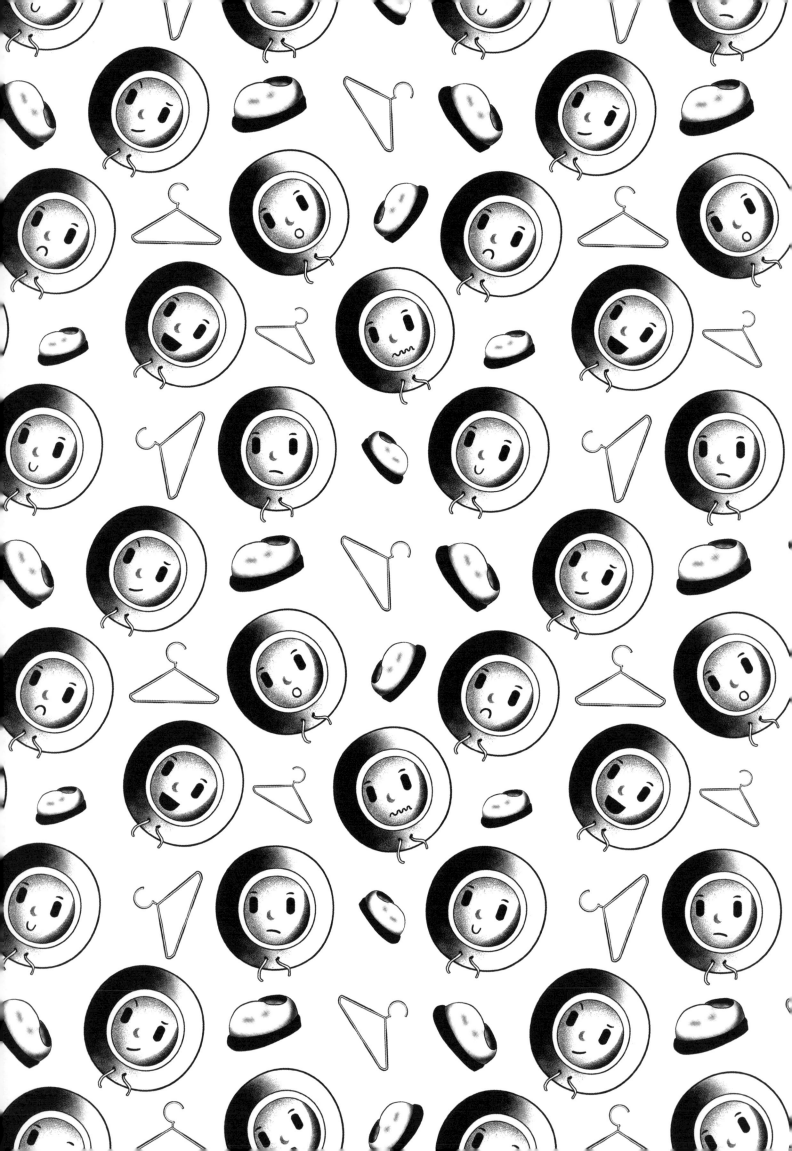

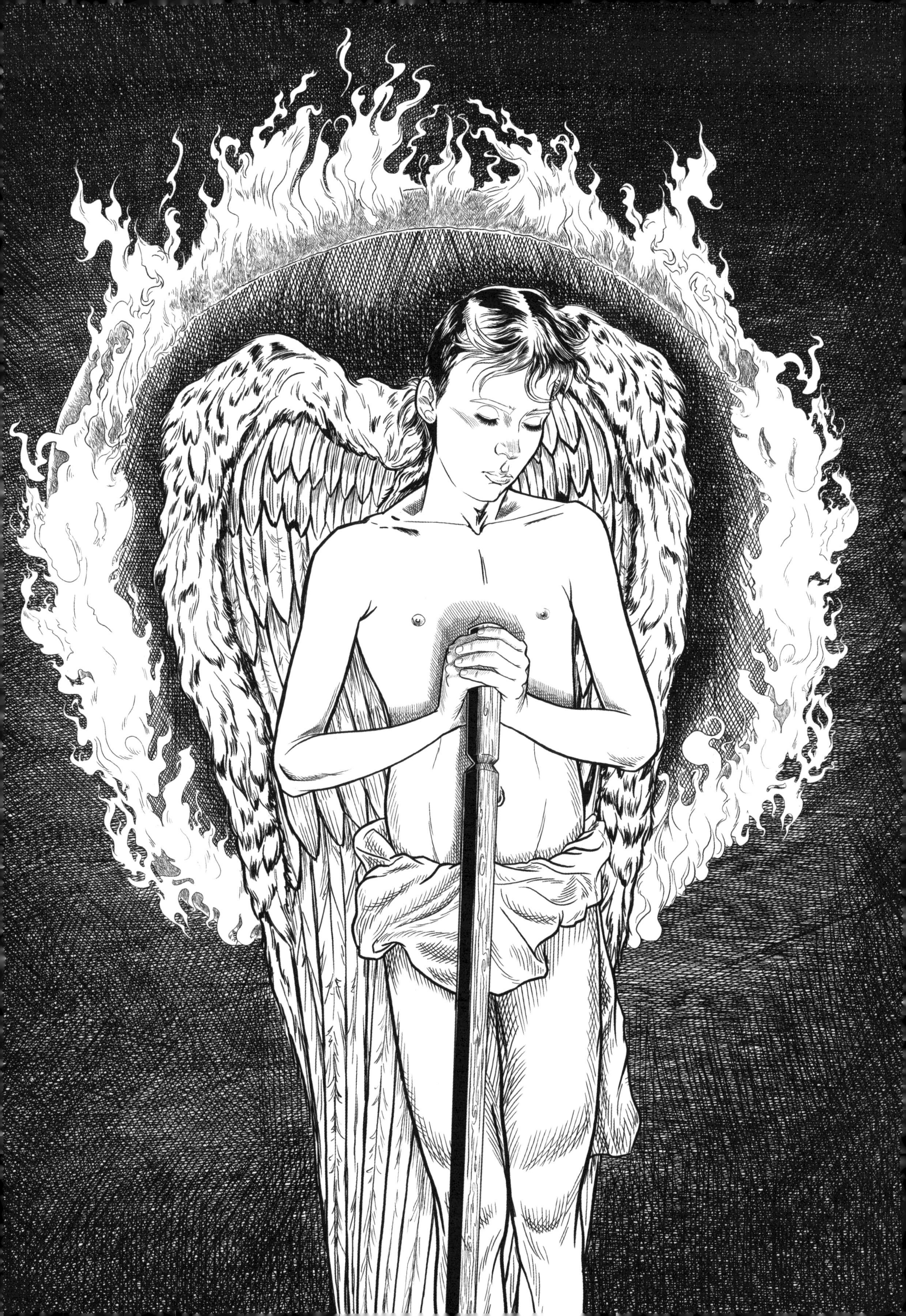

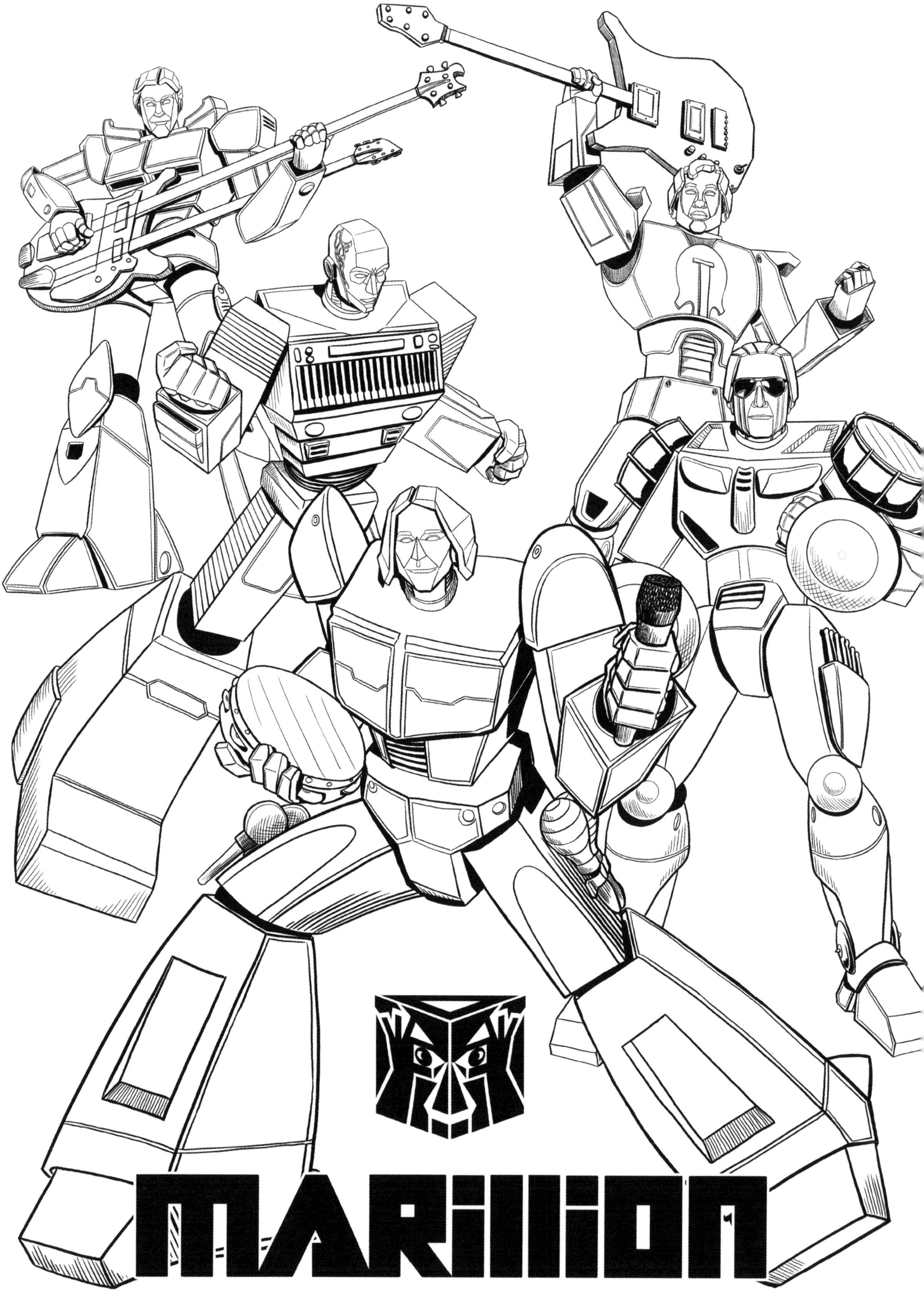
MARILLION

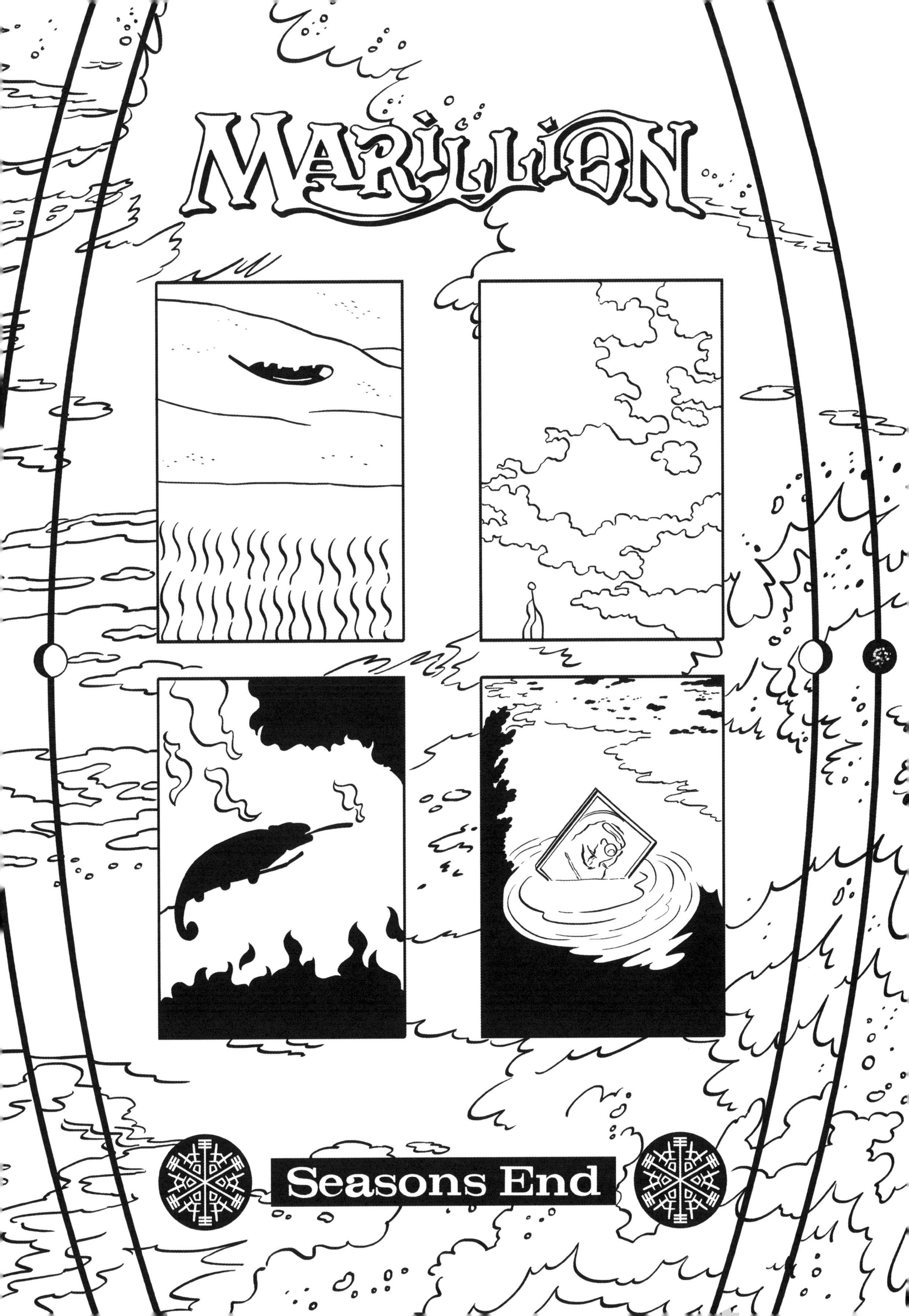
MARILLION
Seasons End

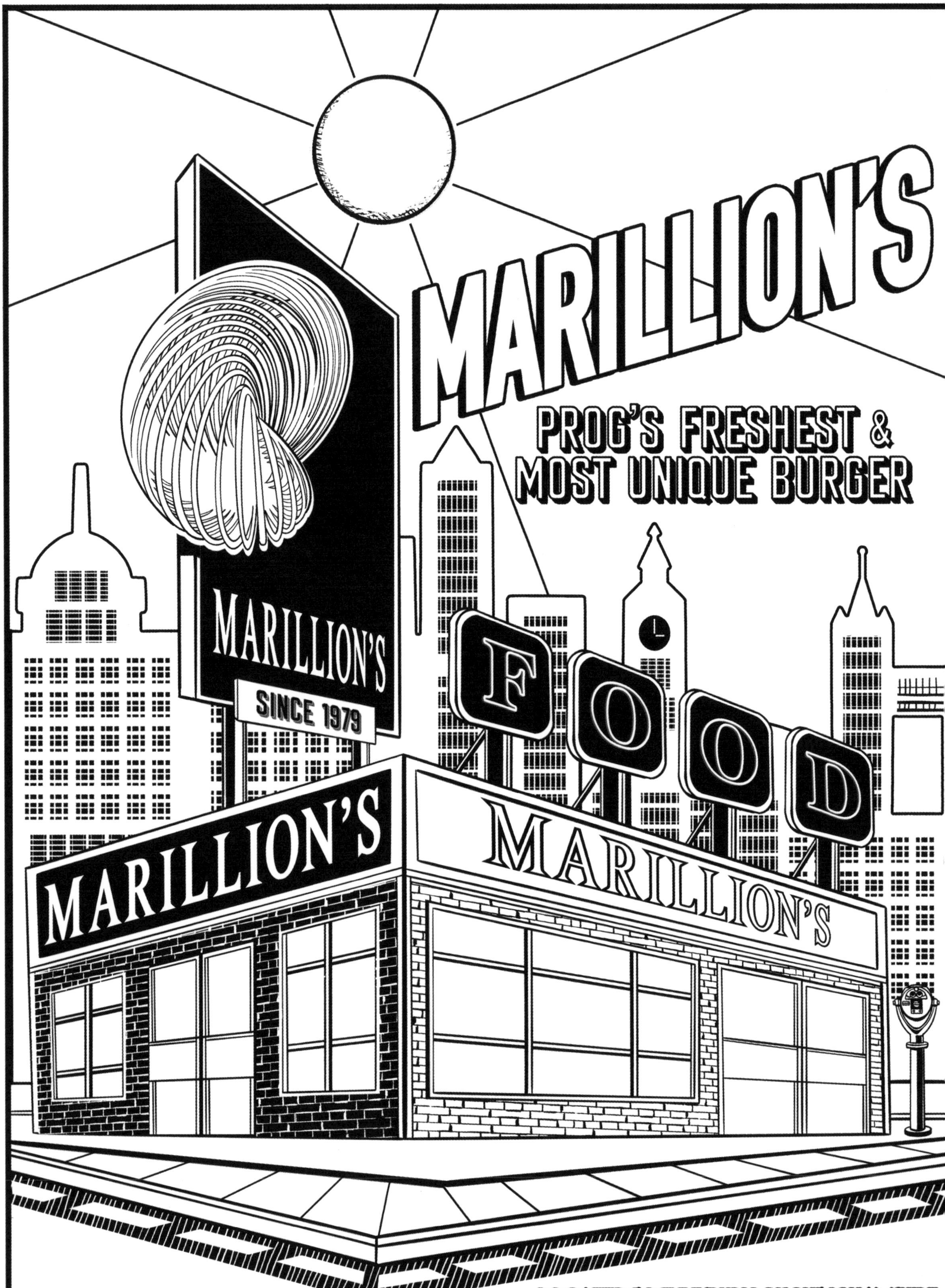
MARILLION'S
PROG'S FRESHEST & MOST UNIQUE BURGER
MARILLION'S
SINCE 1979
FOOD
MARILLION'S
MARILLION'S
LOCATED IN AYLESBURY, BUCKINGHAMSHIRE

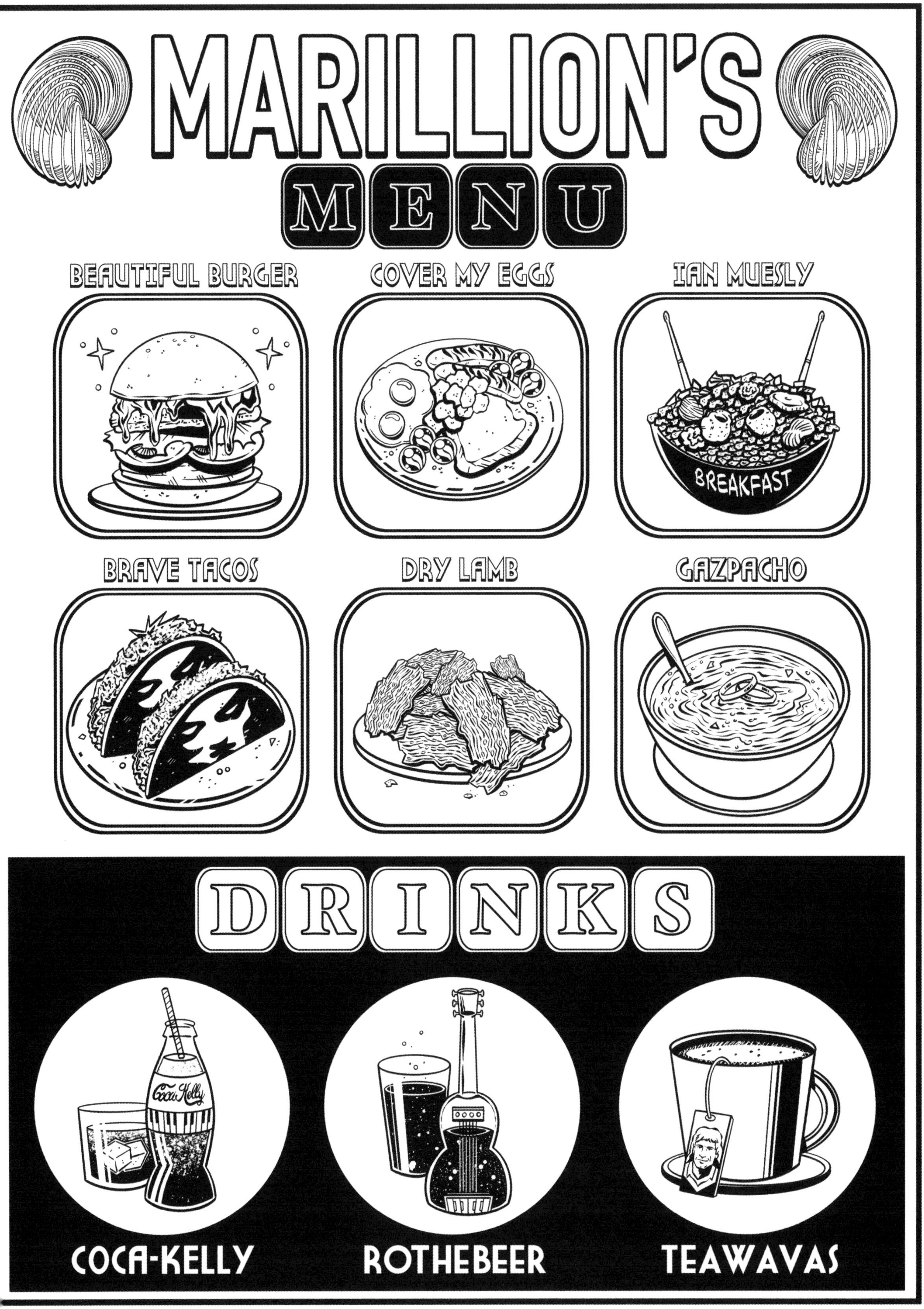
MARILLION'S
MENU
BEAUTIFUL BURGER
COVER MY EGGS
IAN MUESLY
BREAKFAST
BRAVE TACOS
DRY LAMB
GAZPACHO
DRINKS
Coca-Kelly
COCA-KELLY
ROTHEBEER
TEAWAVAS

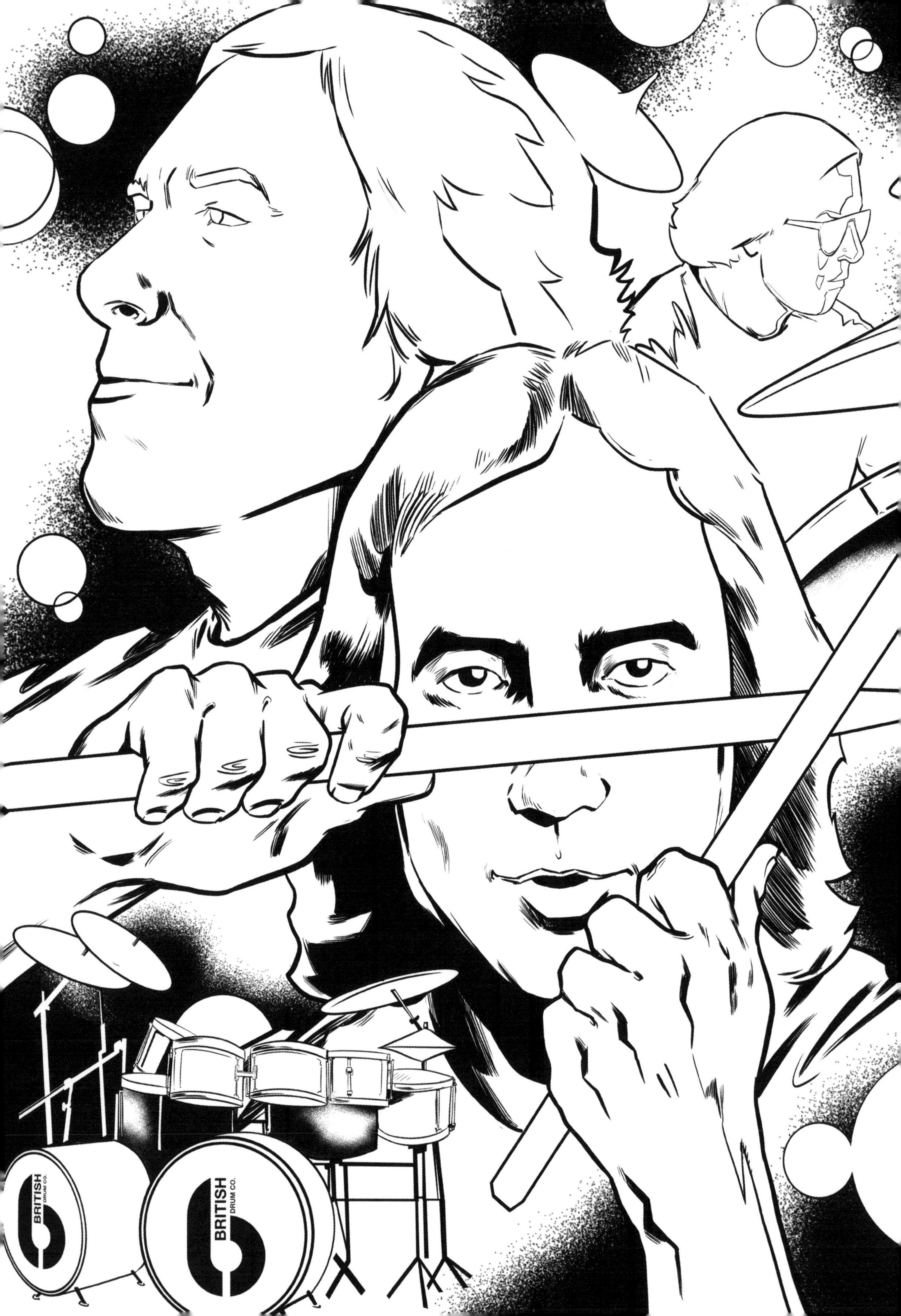
BRITISH DRUM CO.
BRITISH DRUM CO.

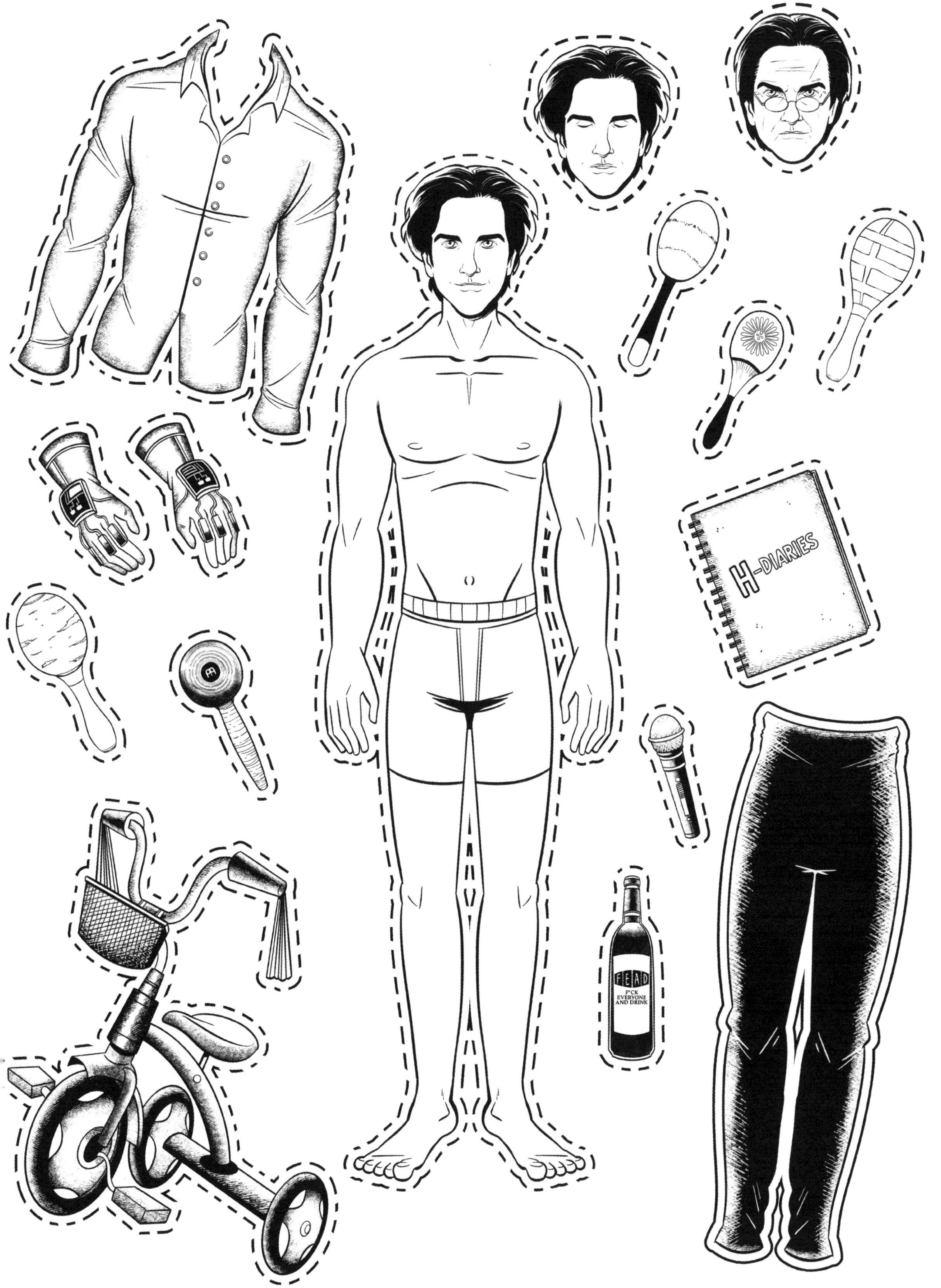
H-DIARIES
FEAD
F*CK
EVERYONE
AND DRINK

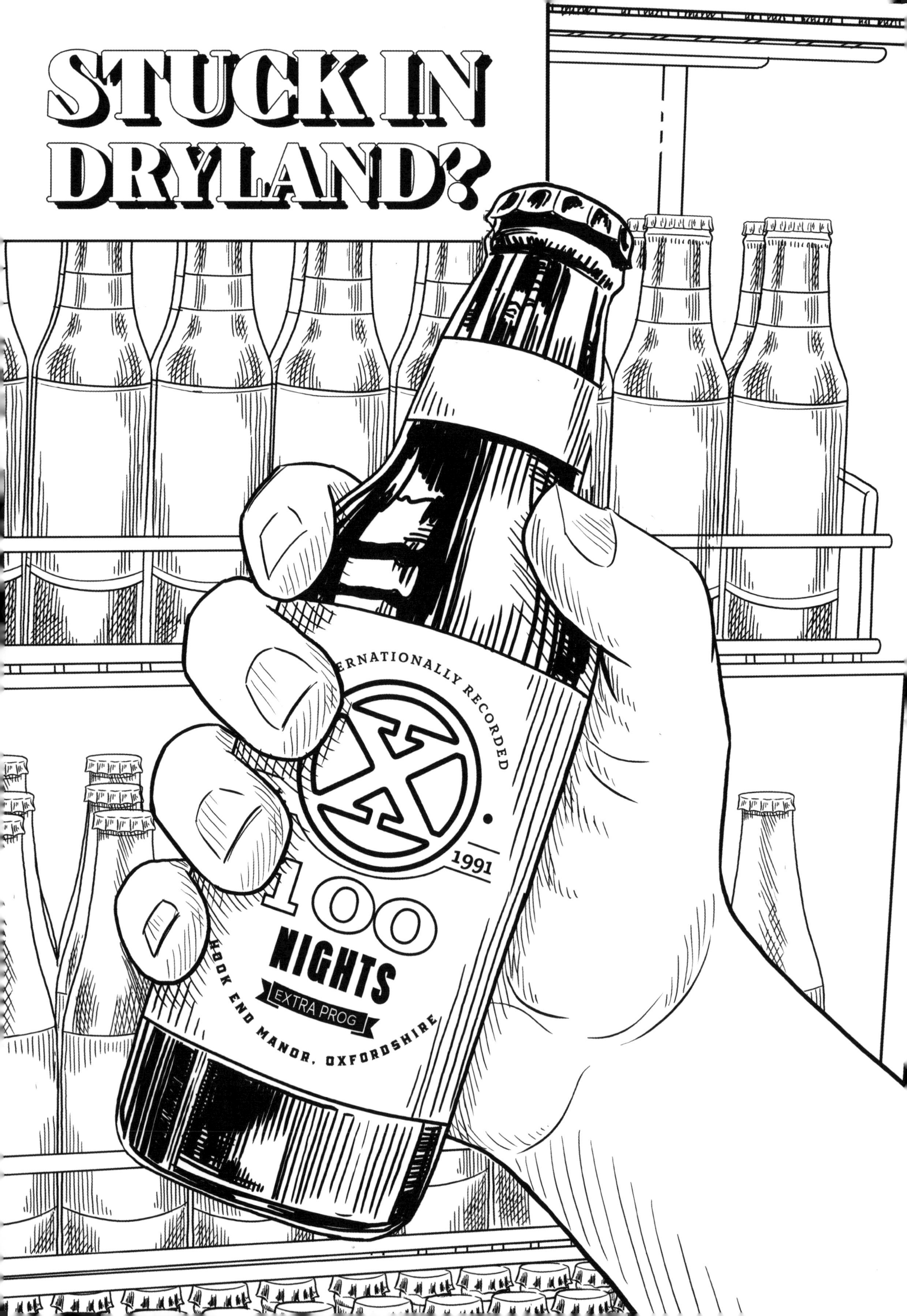
STUCK IN DRYLAND?
ERNATIONALLY RECORDED
1991
100
NIGHTS
EXTRA PROG
HOOK END MANOR, OXFORDSHIRE

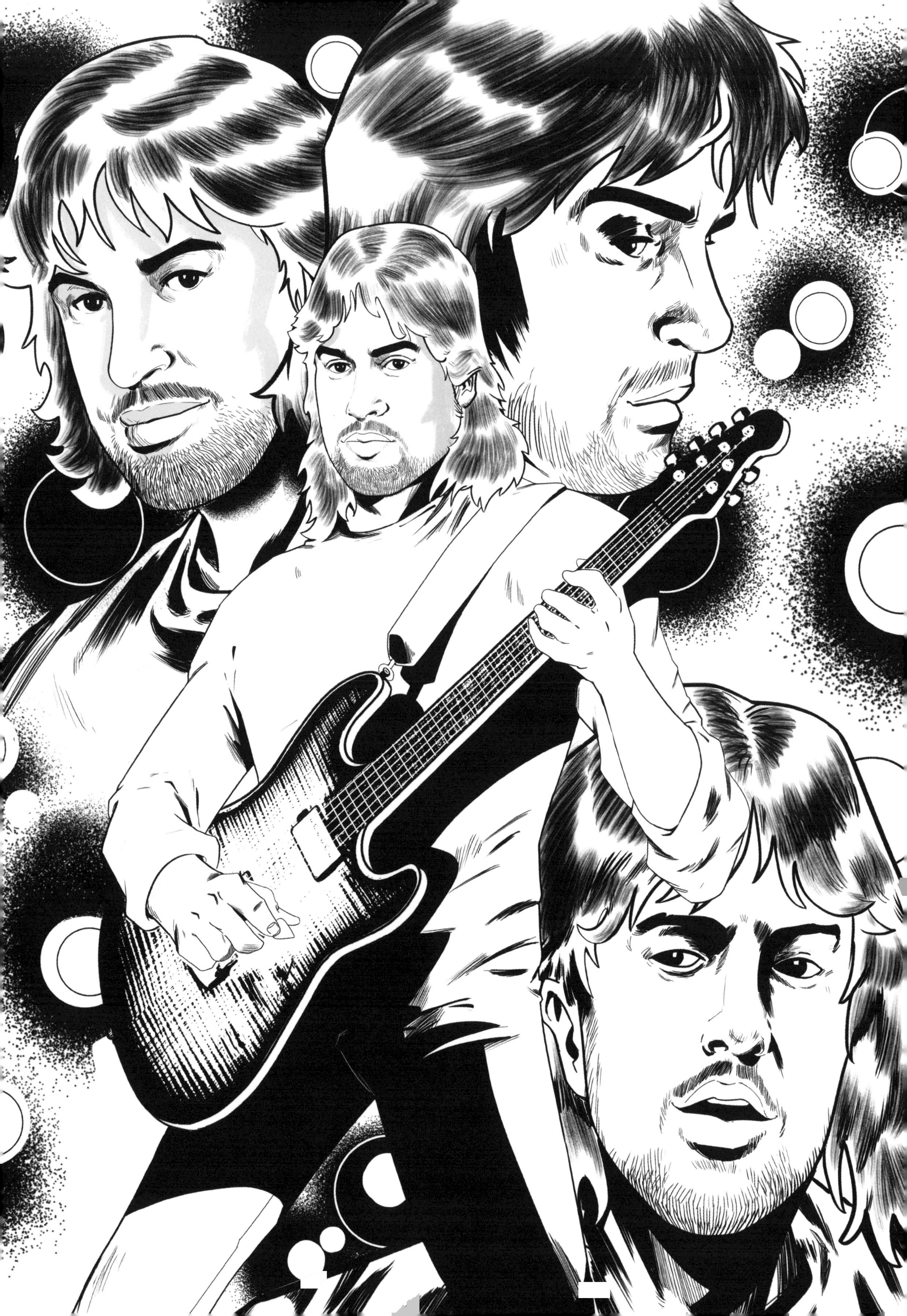

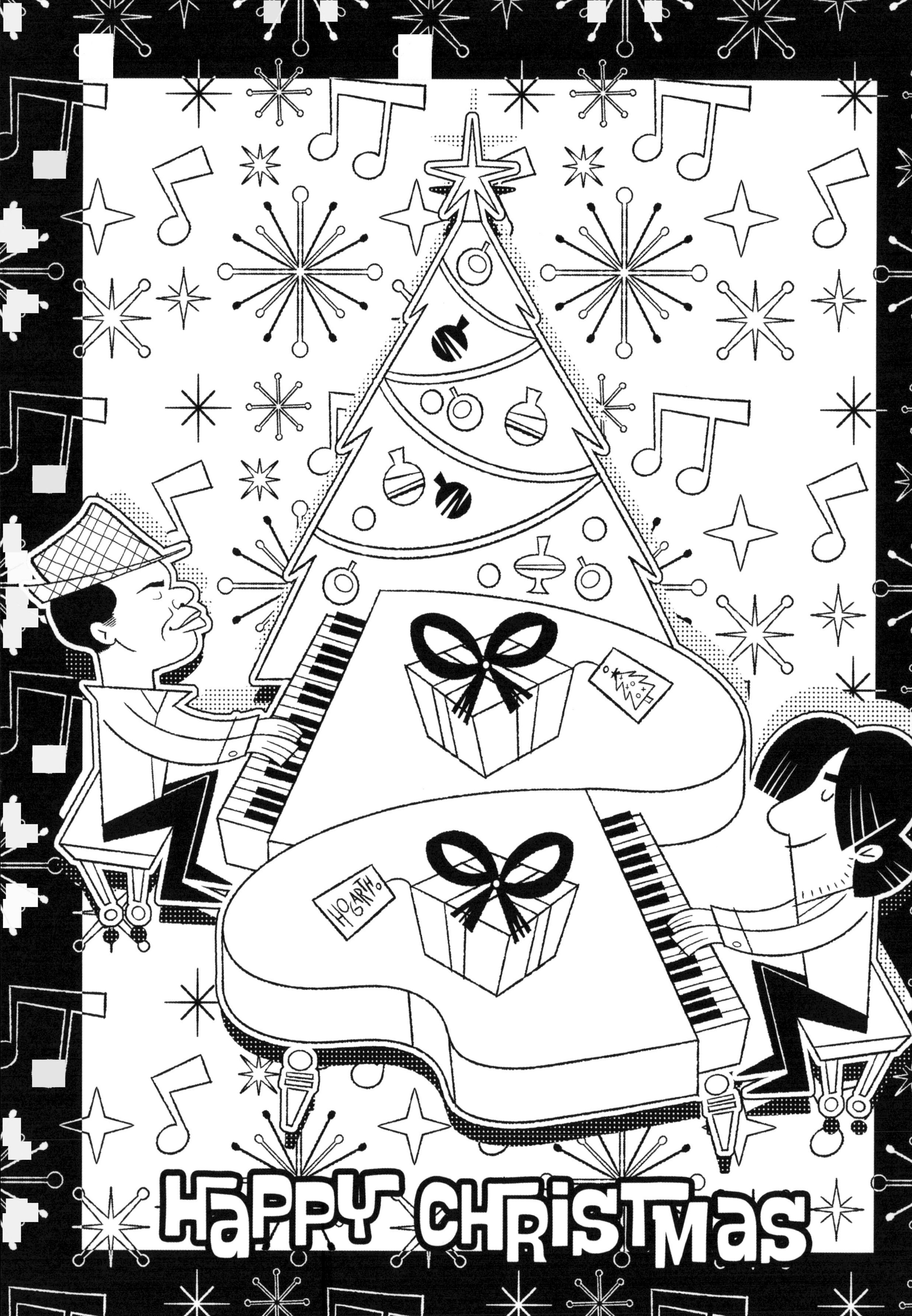
HOGARTH.
HAPPY CHRISTMAS

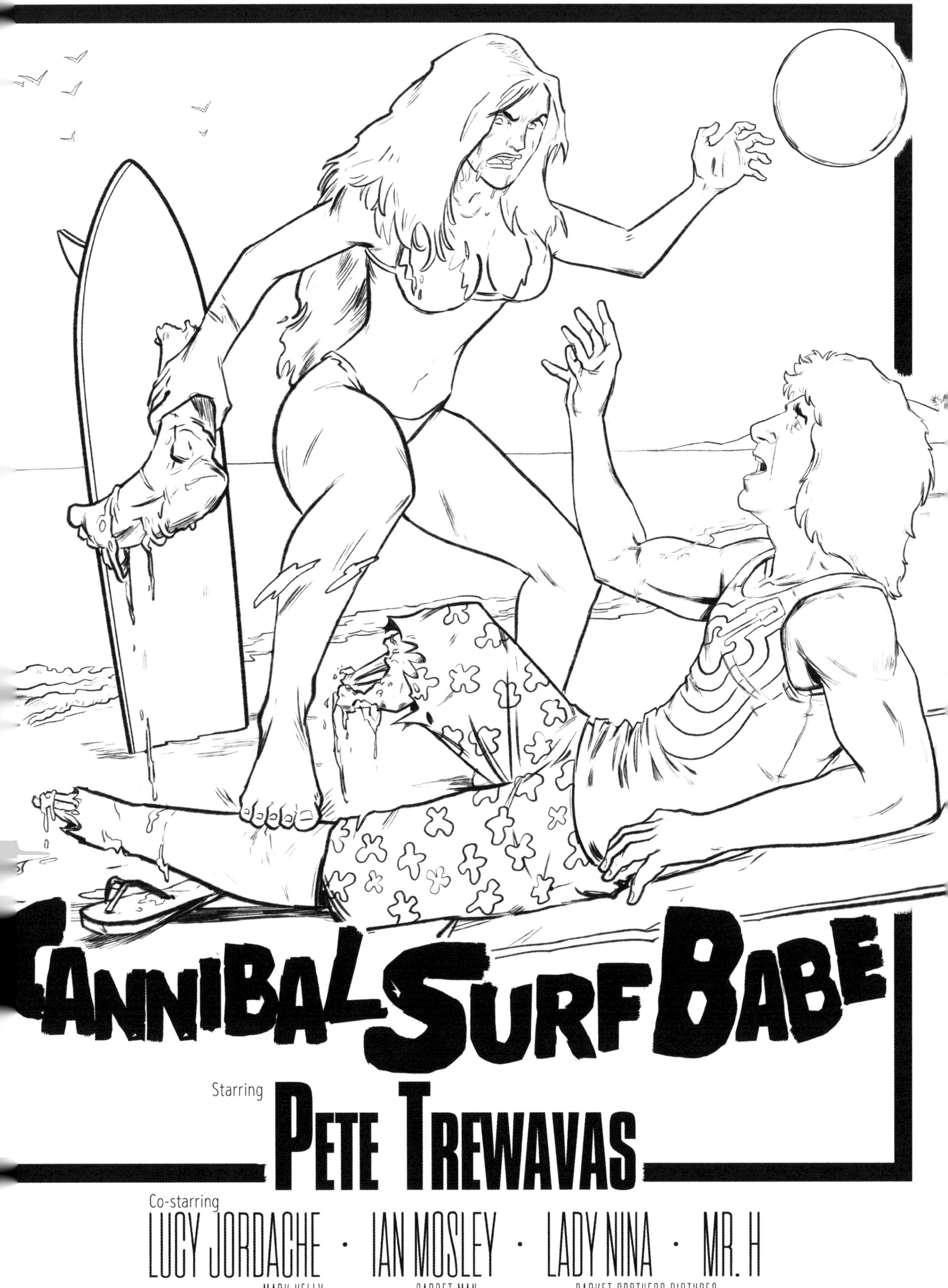
CANNIBAL SURF BABE
Starring
PETE TREWAVAS
Co-starring
LUCY JORDACHE · IAN MOSLEY · LADY NINA · MR. H
Written by: MARK KELLY · Directed by: GADGET MAN · Produced by: RACKET BROTHERS PICTURES

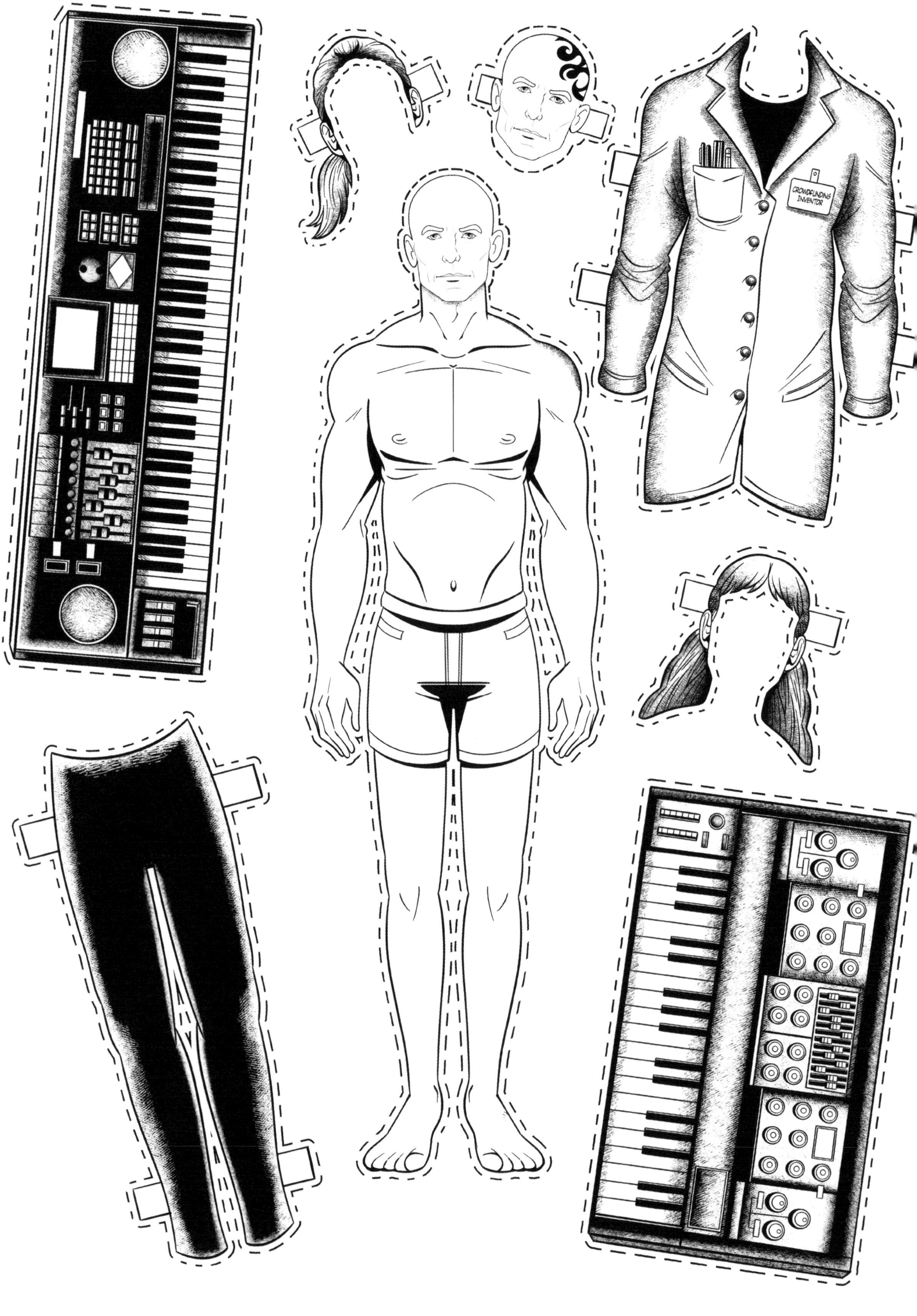
CROWDFUNDING INVENTOR

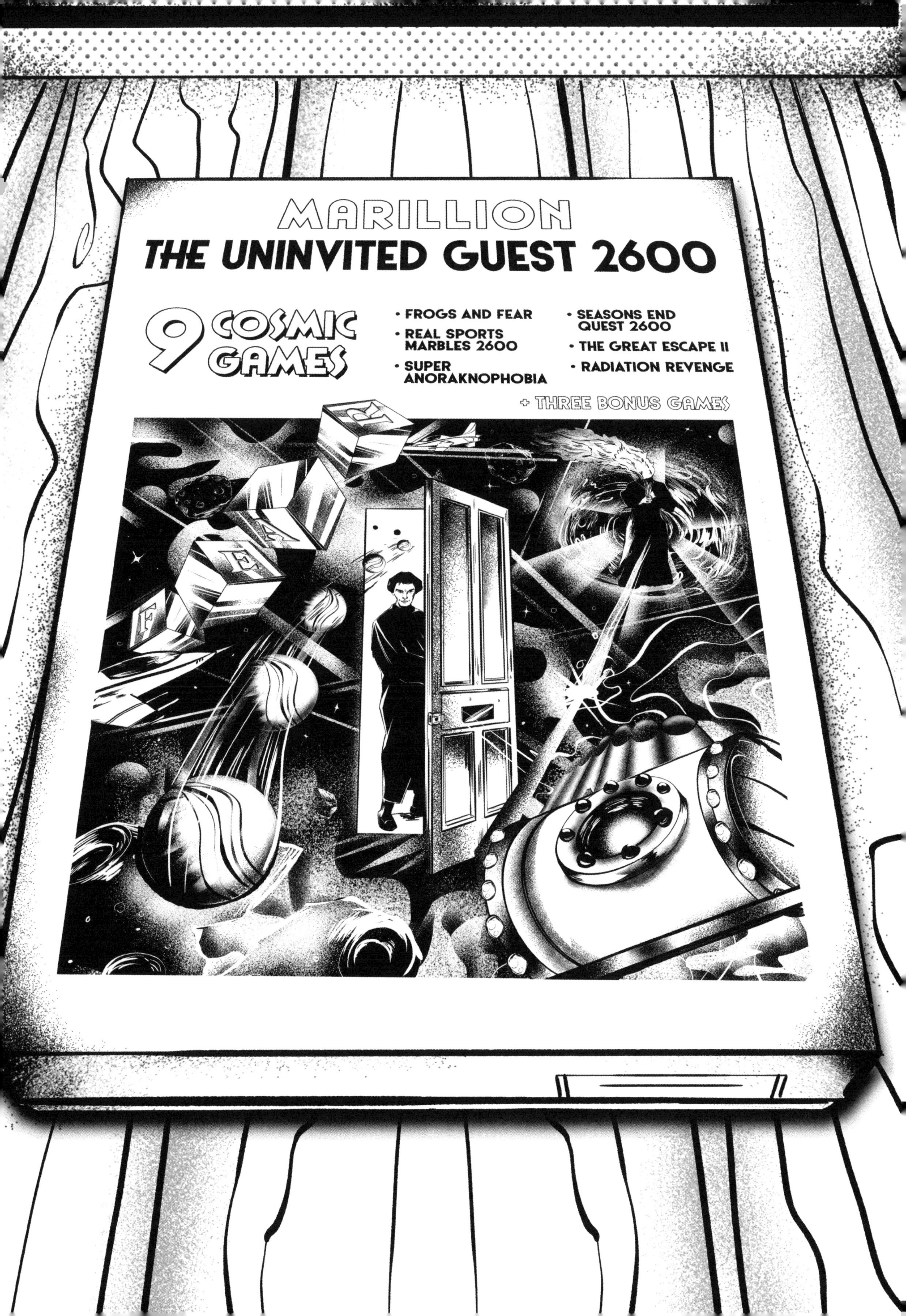
MARILLION
THE UNINVITED GUEST 2600
9 COSMIC GAMES
• FROGS AND FEAR
• REAL SPORTS MARBLES 2600
• SUPER ANORAKNOPHOBIA
• SEASONS END QUEST 2600
• THE GREAT ESCAPE II
• RADIATION REVENGE
+ THREE BONUS GAMES

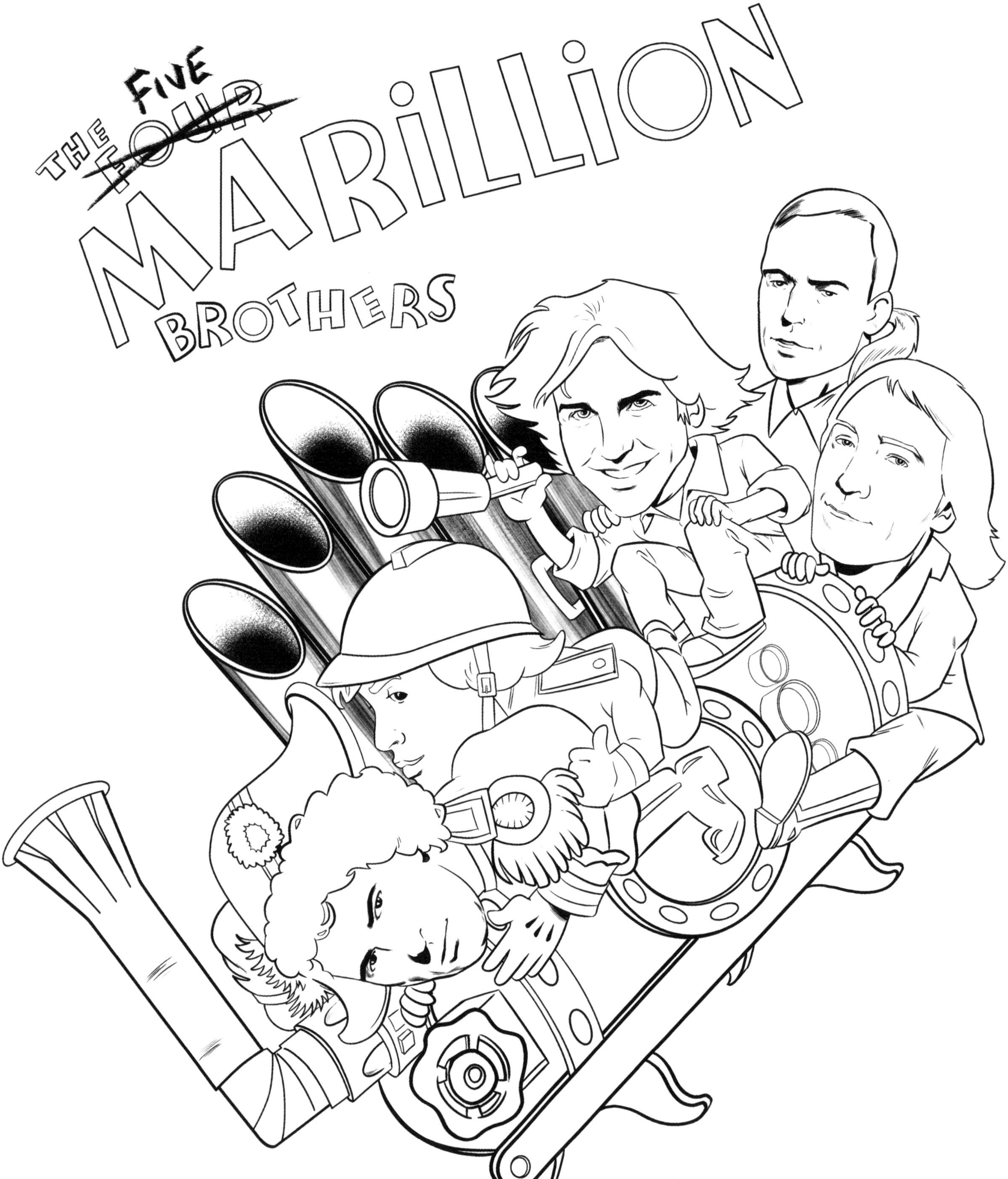
THE ~~FOUR~~ FIVE
MARILLION
BROTHERS

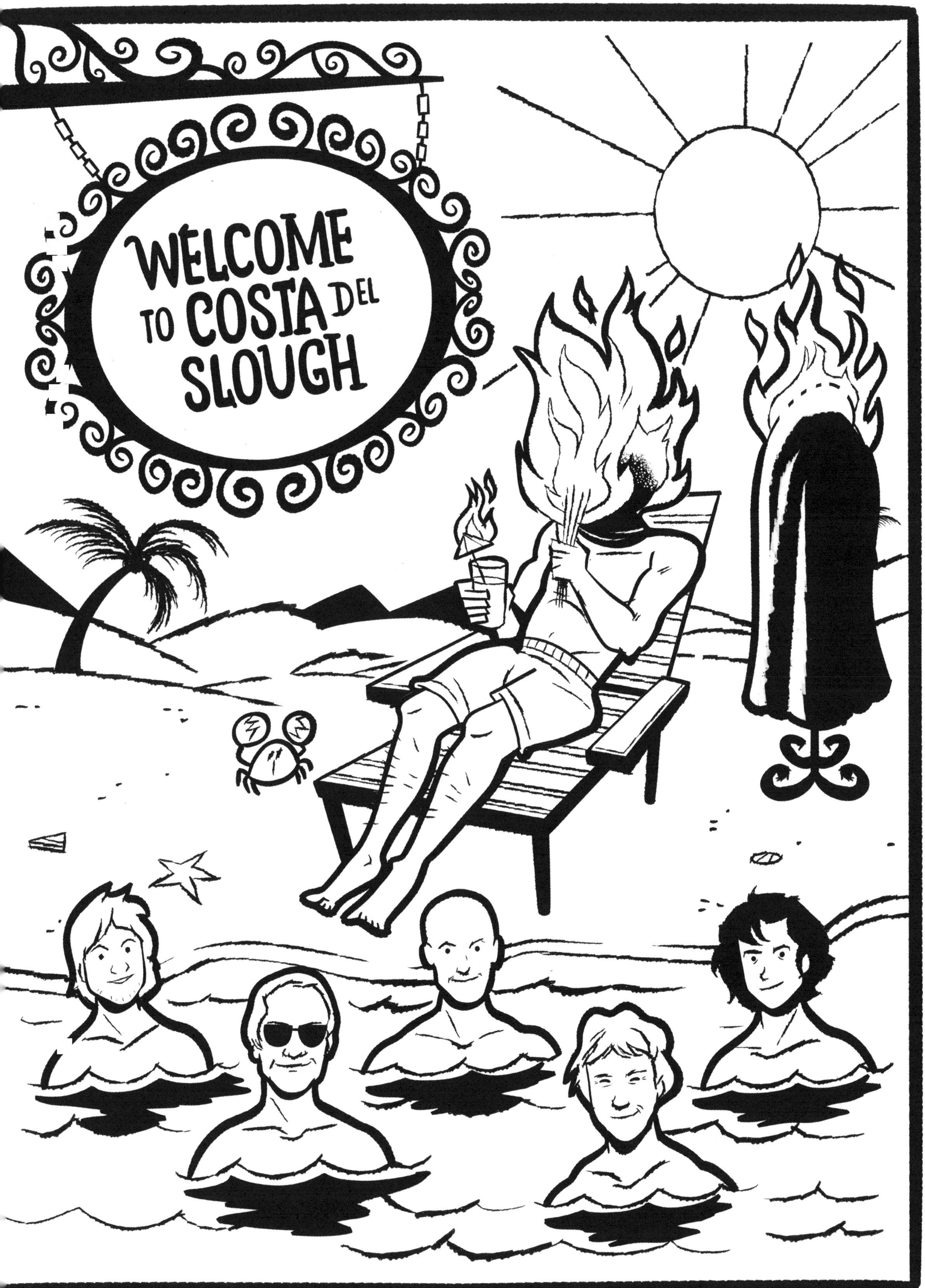
WELCOME TO COSTA DEL SLOUGH

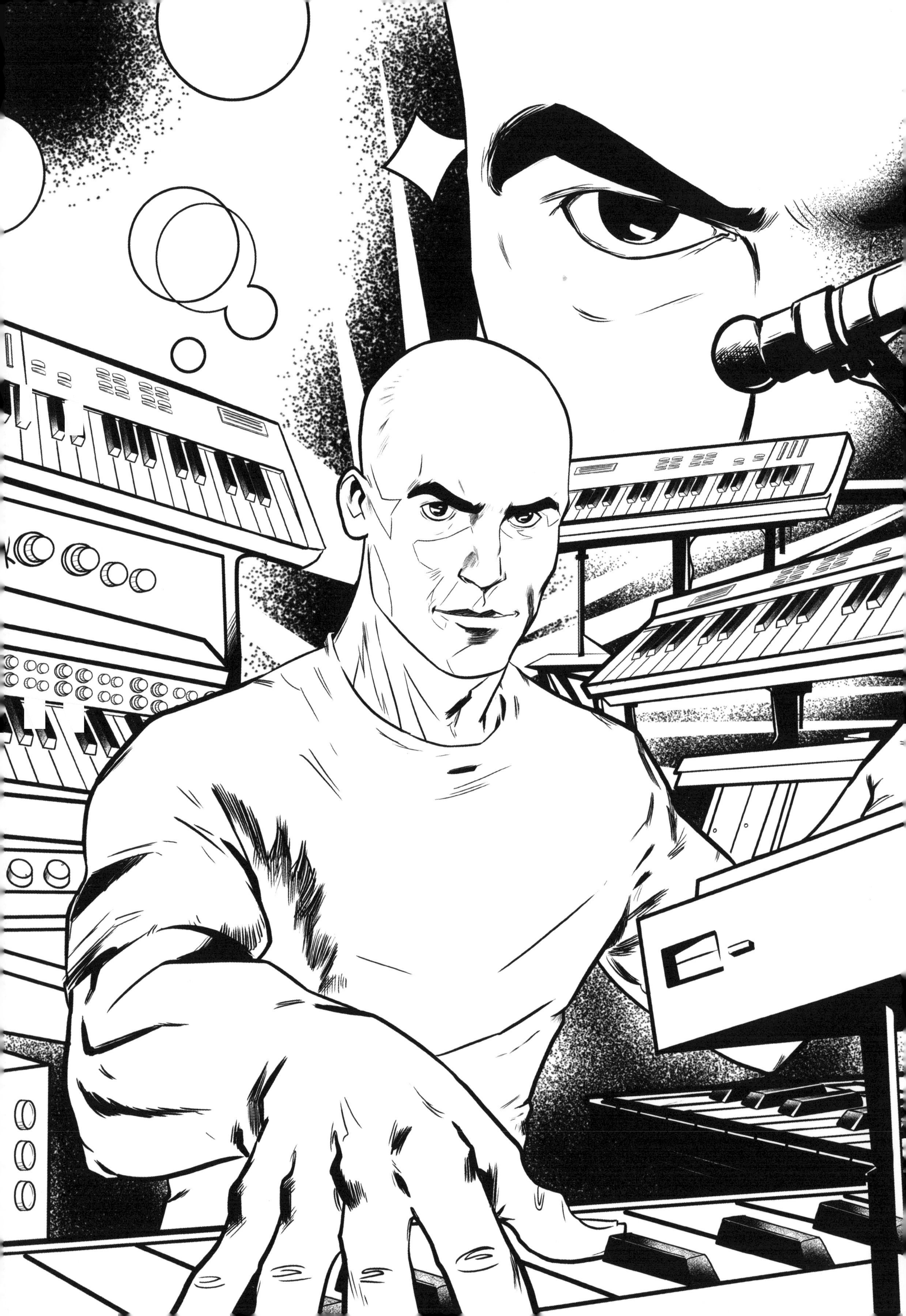

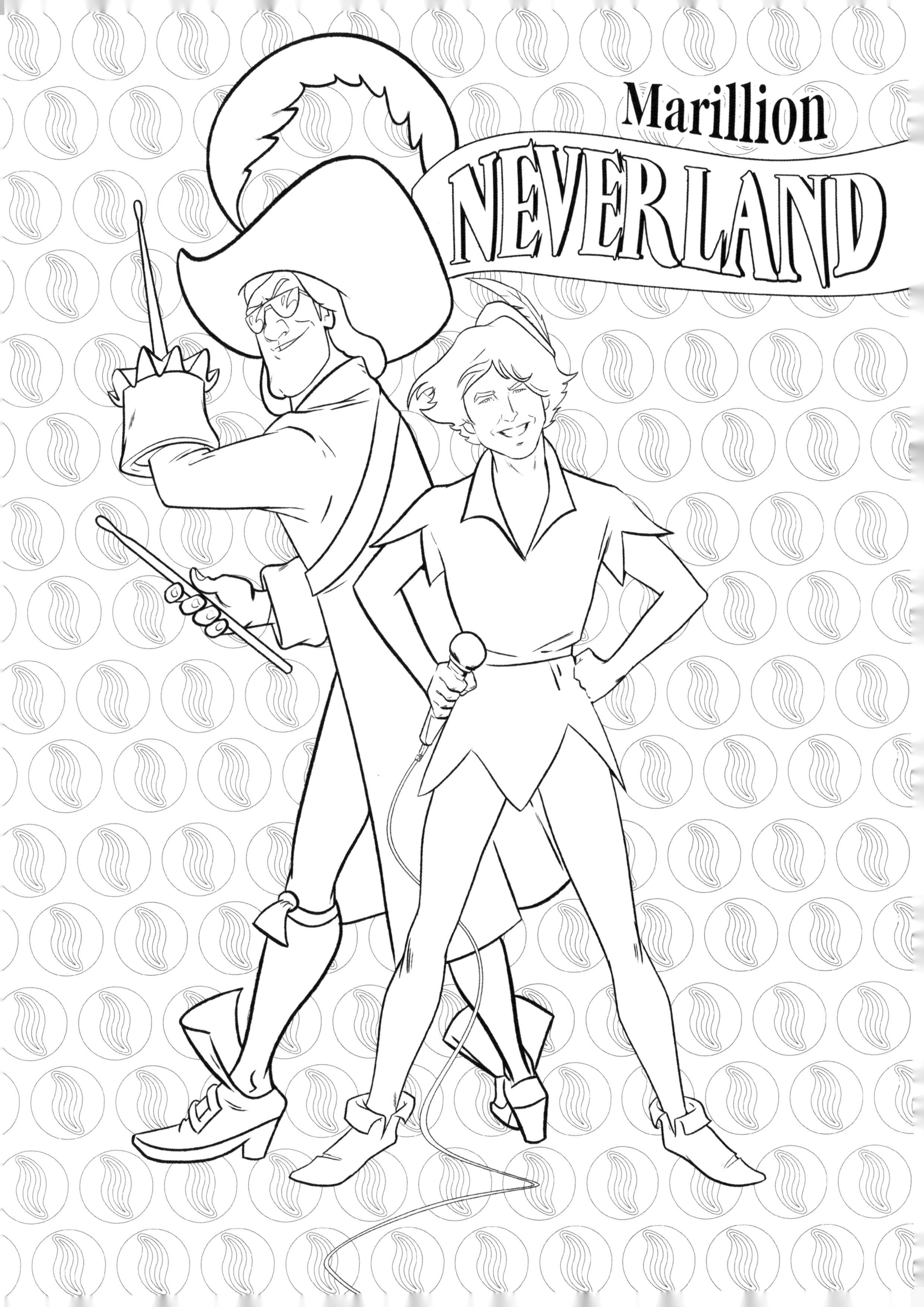
Marillion
NEVERLAND

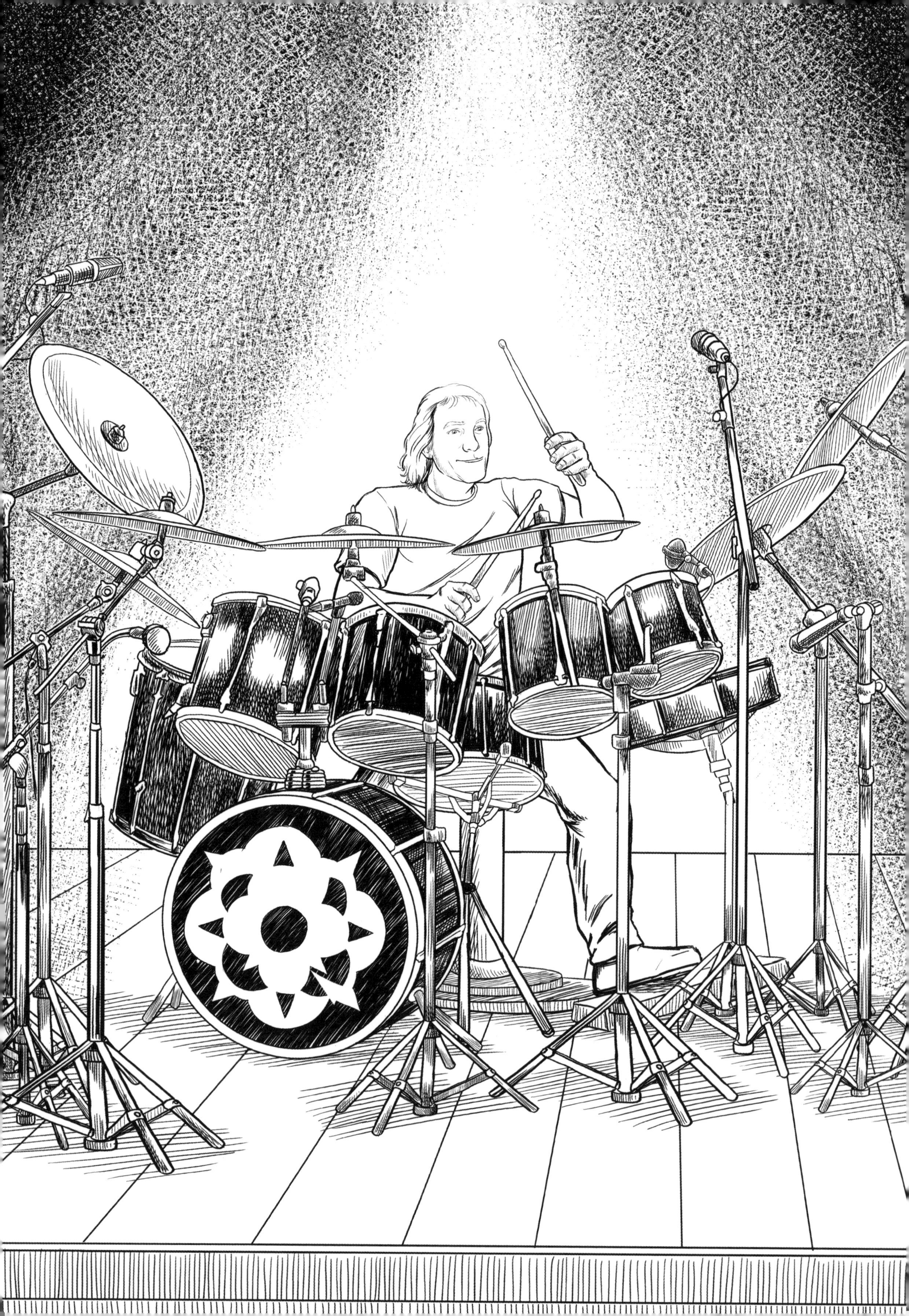

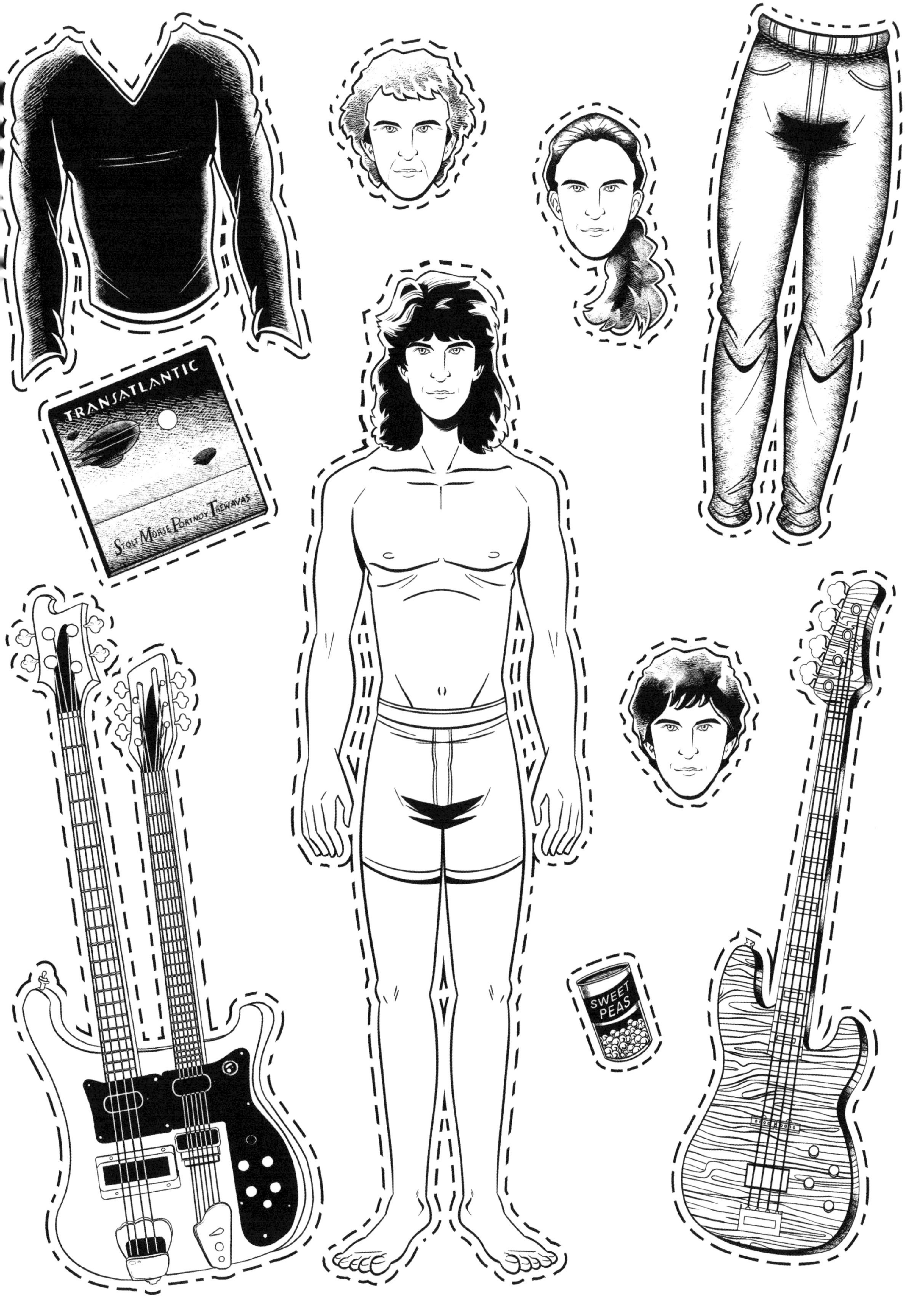
TRANSATLANTIC
STOLT MORSE PORTNOY TREWAVAS
SWEET PEAS

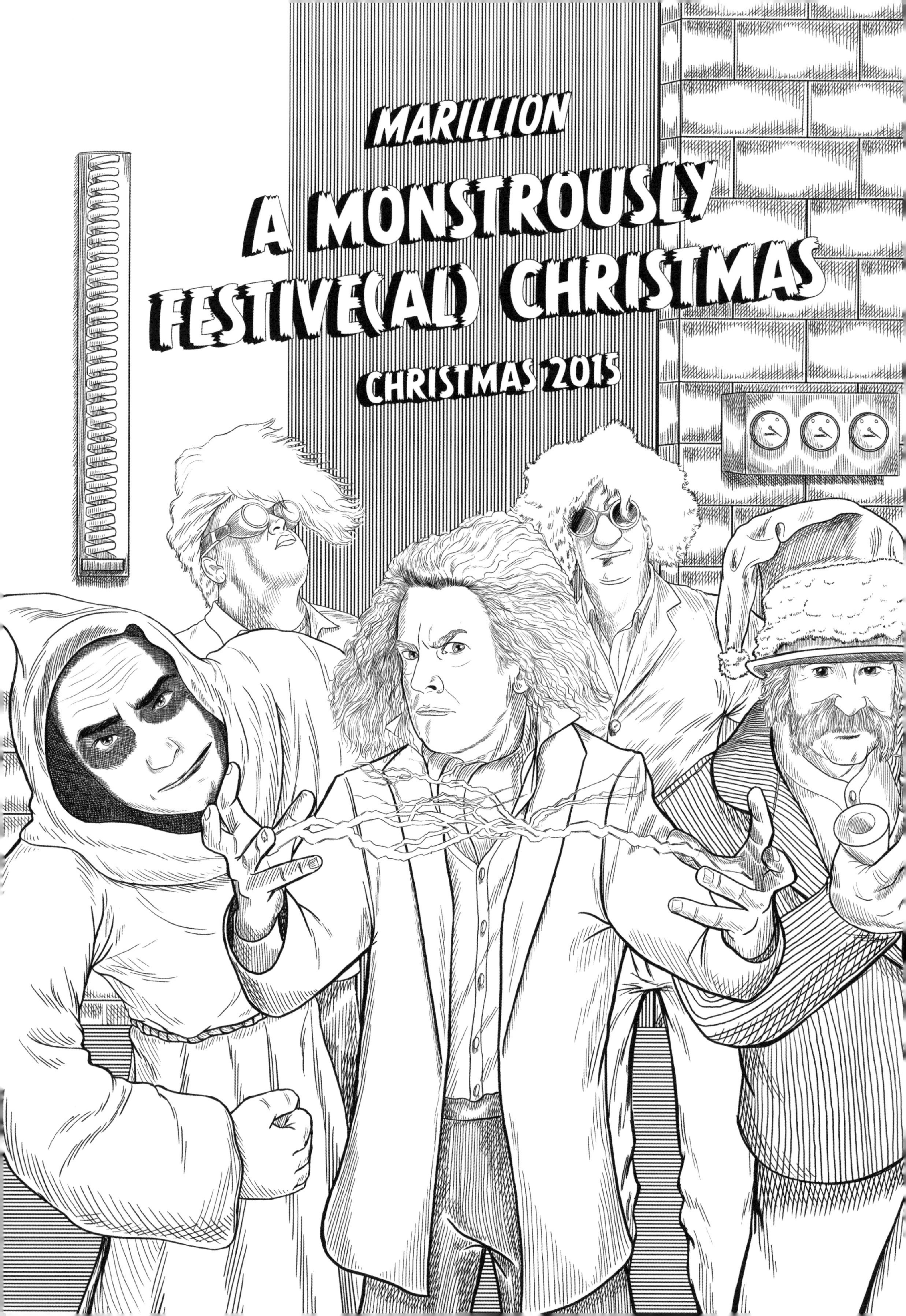
MARILLION
A MONSTROUSLY FESTIVE(AL) CHRISTMAS
CHRISTMAS 2015

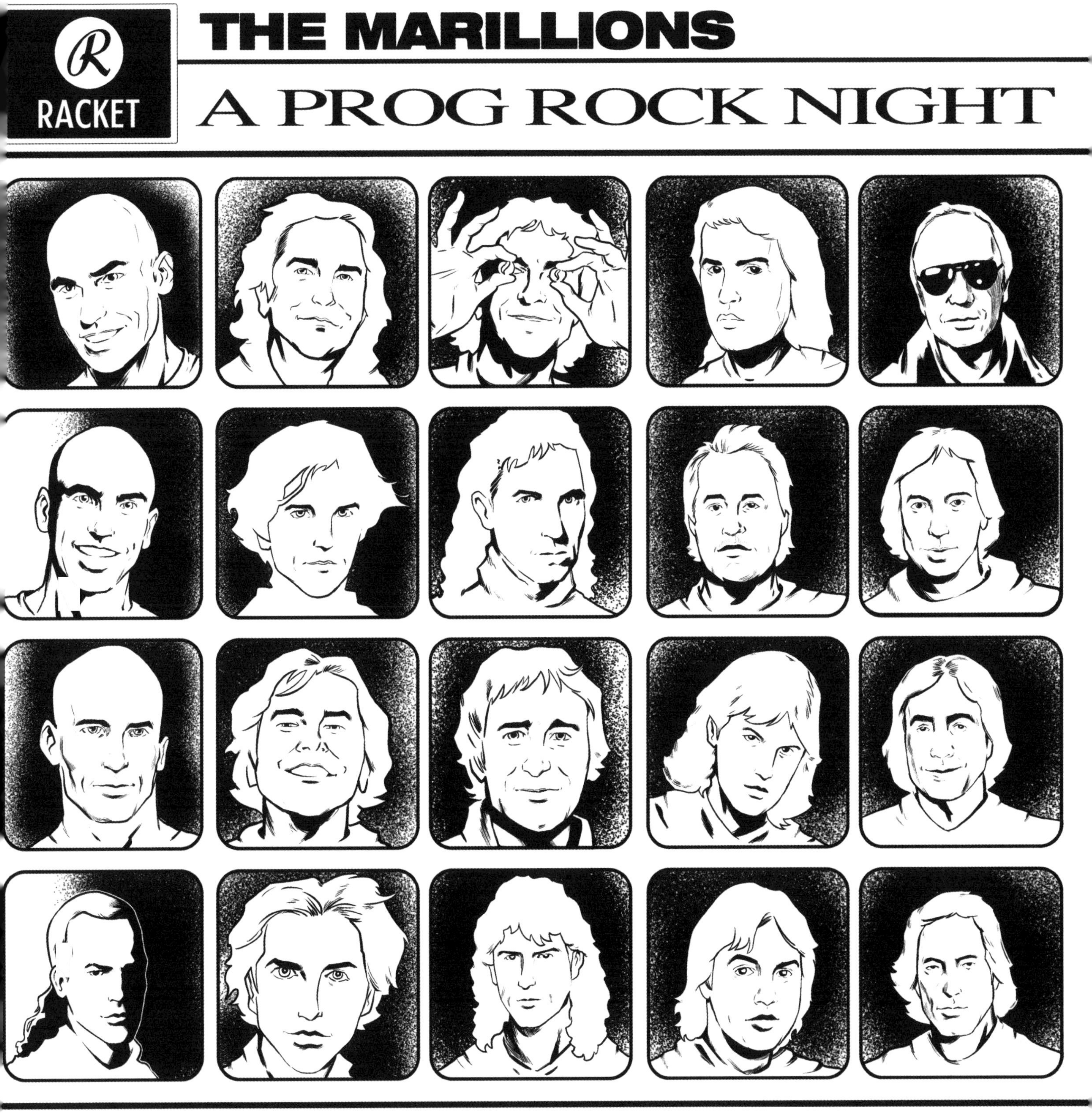
R
RACKET
THE MARILLIONS
A PROG ROCK NIGHT

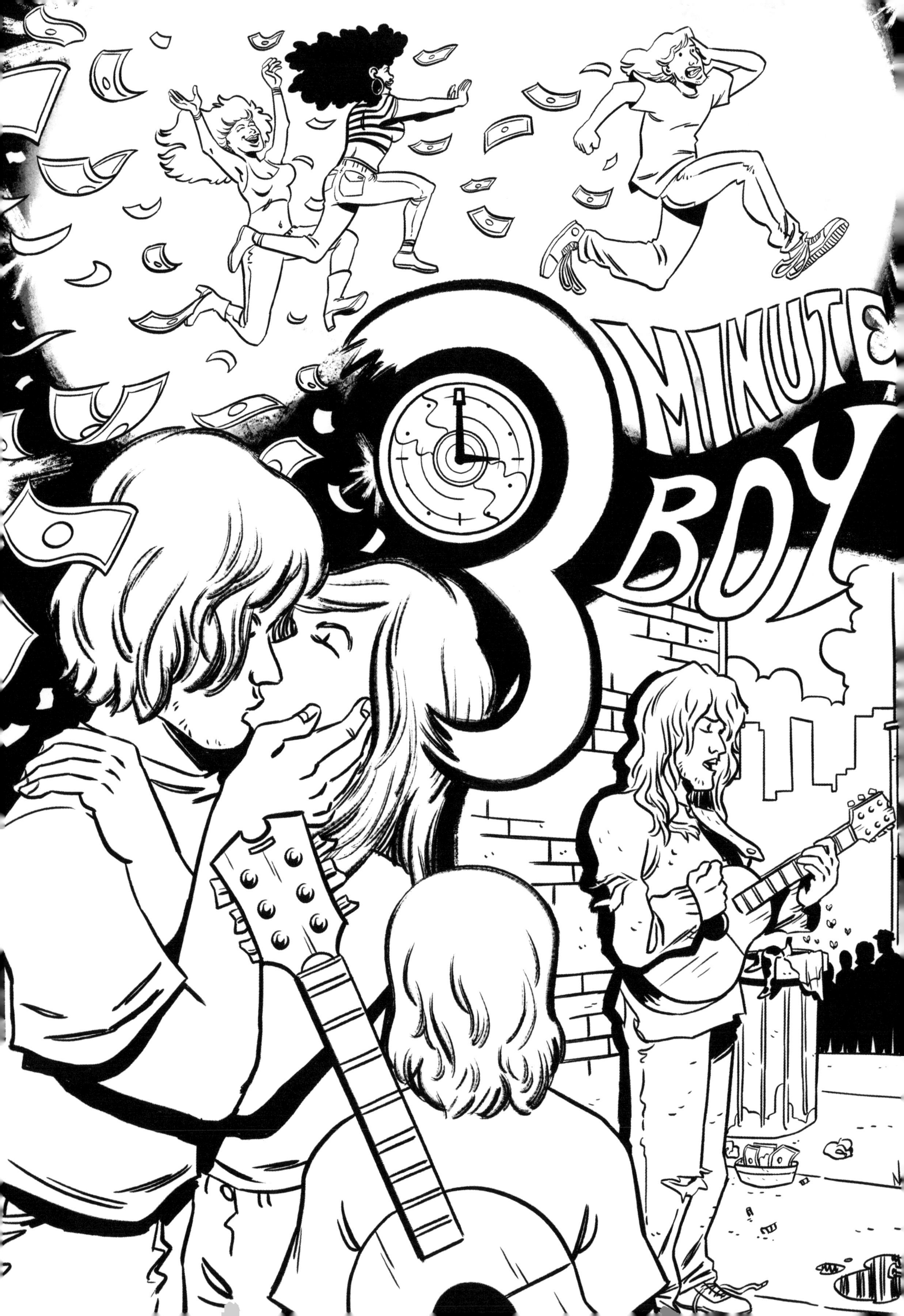
3 MINUTE
BOY

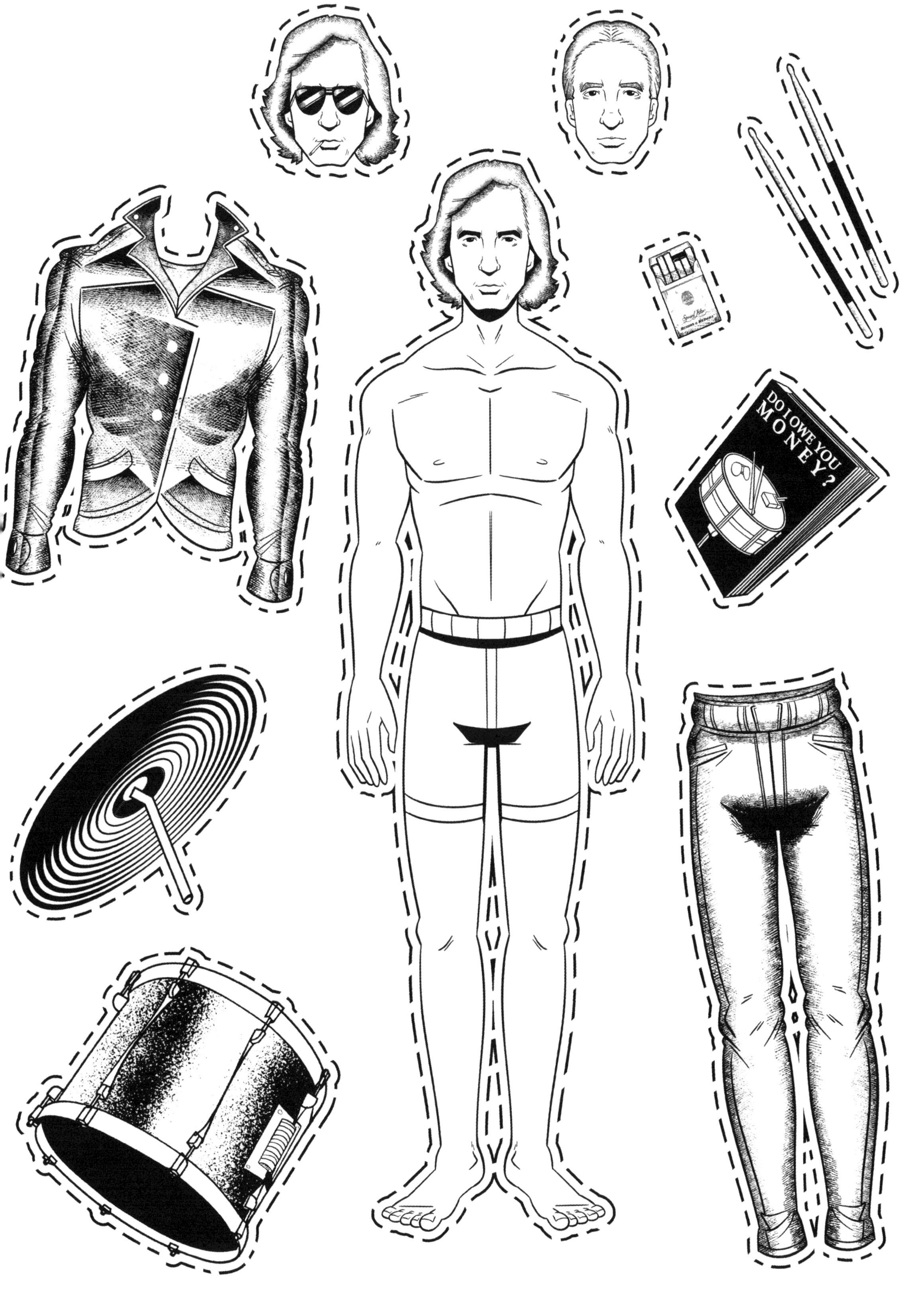
DO I OWE YOU
MONEY?

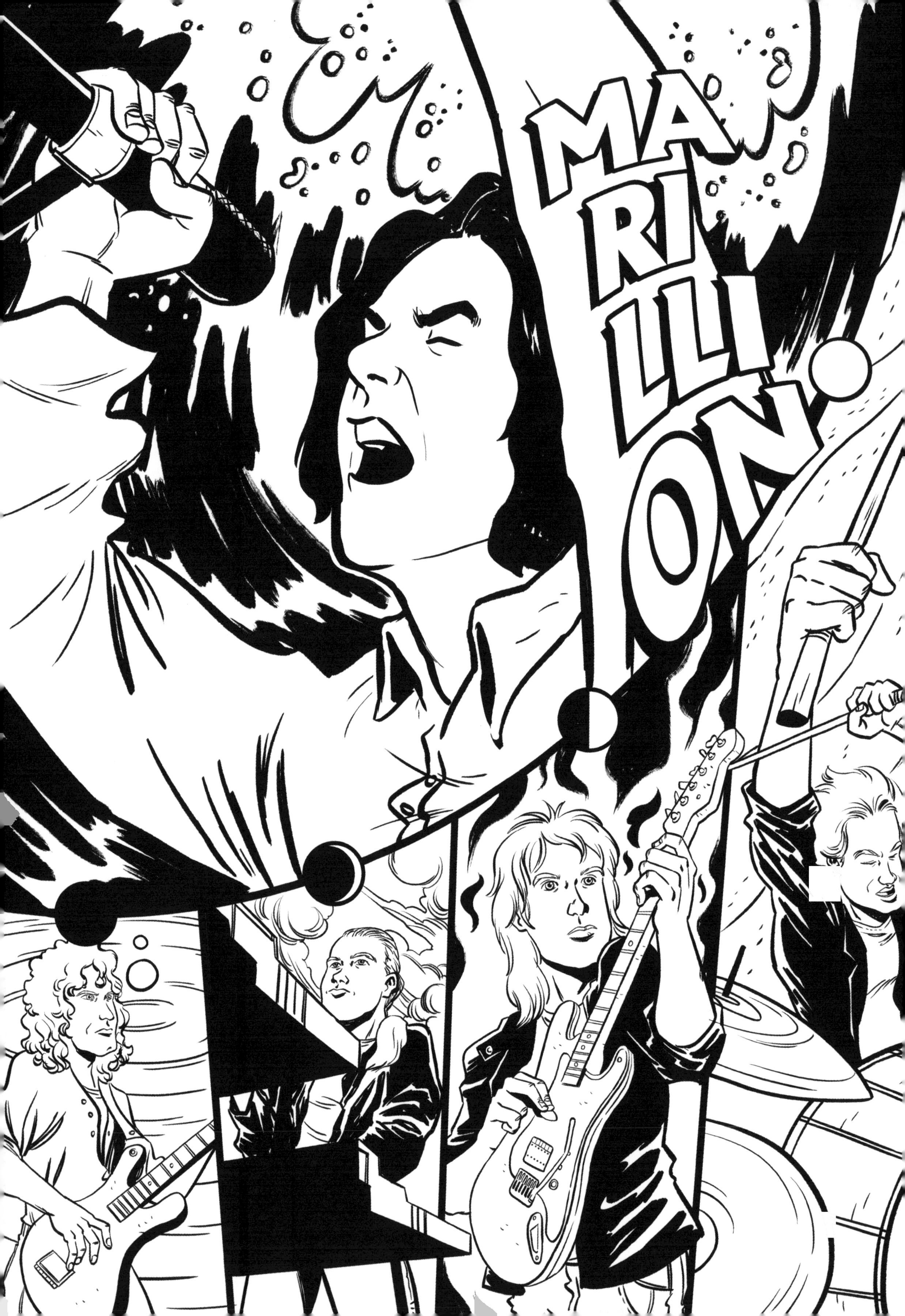
MA RI LLI ON!

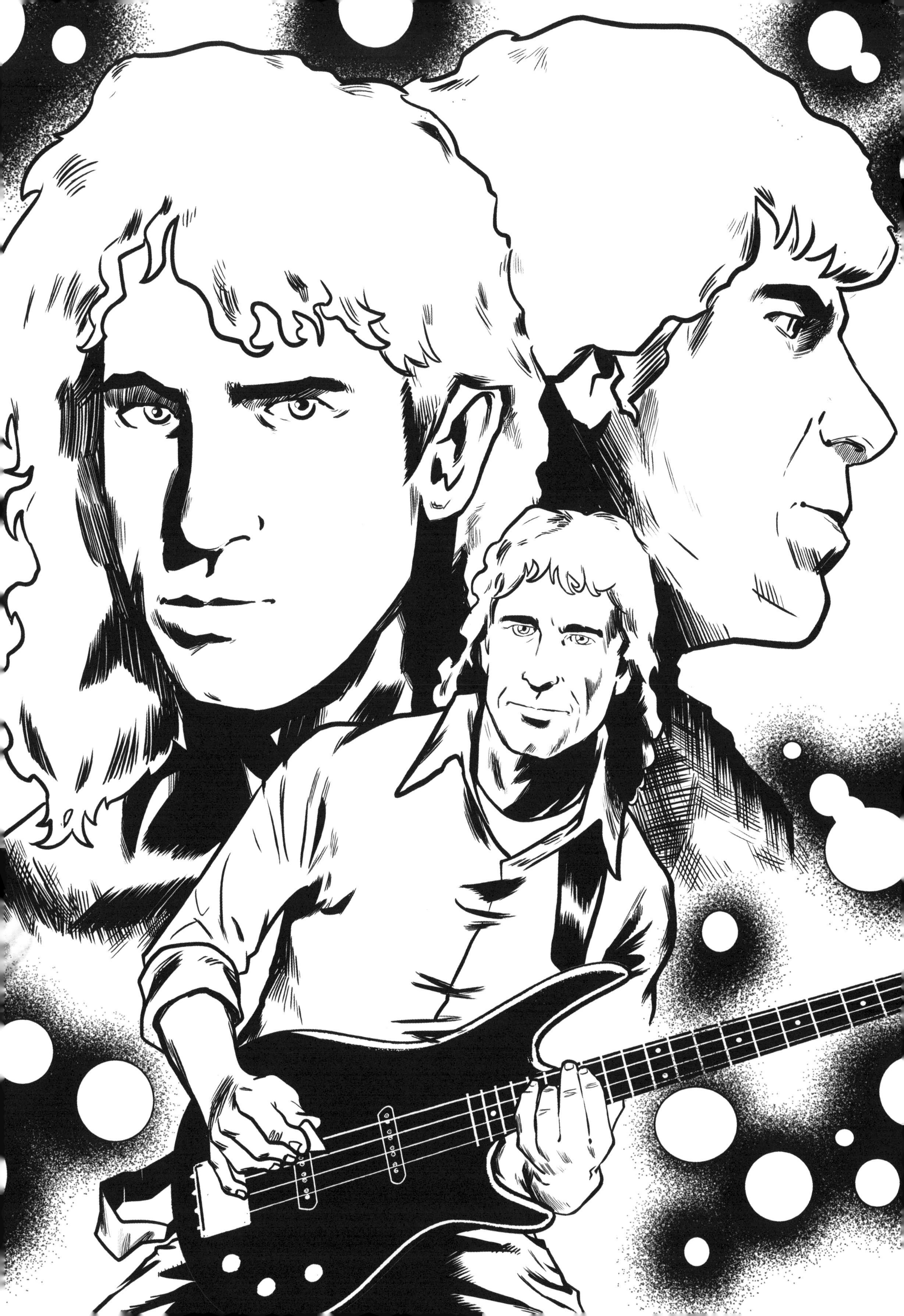

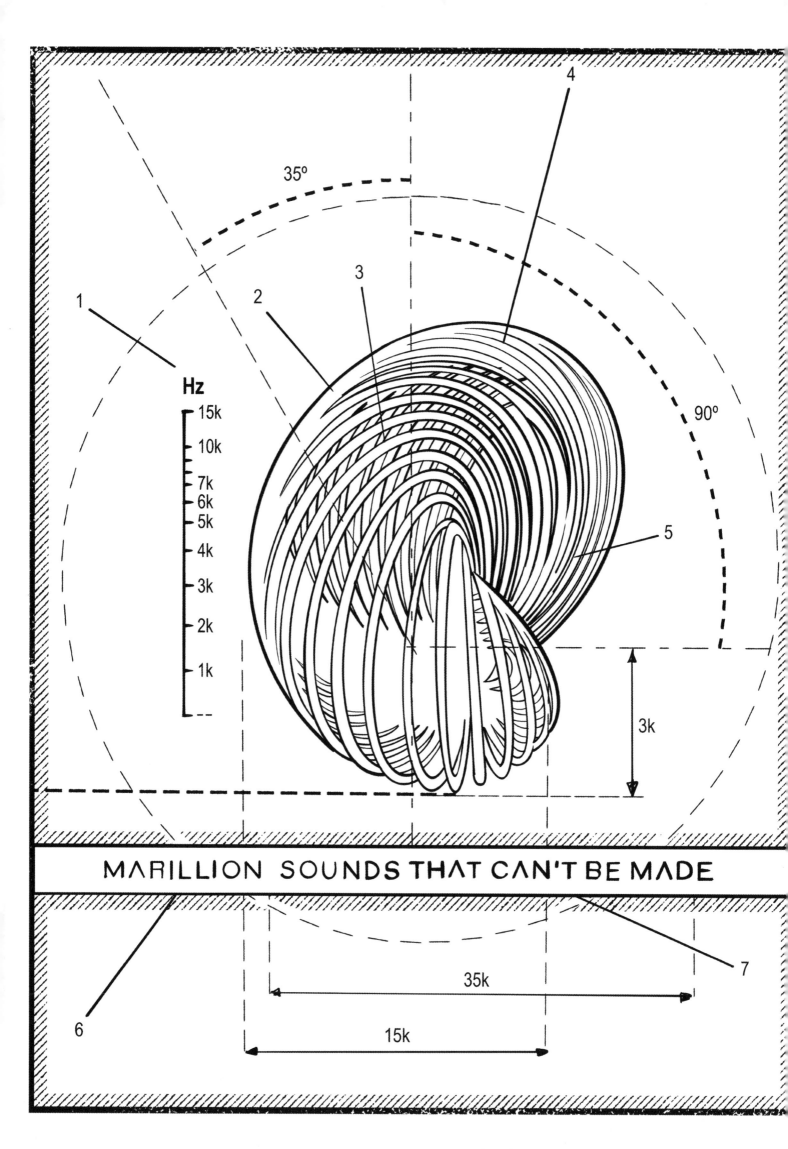

MARILLION SOUNDS THAT CAN'T BE MADE

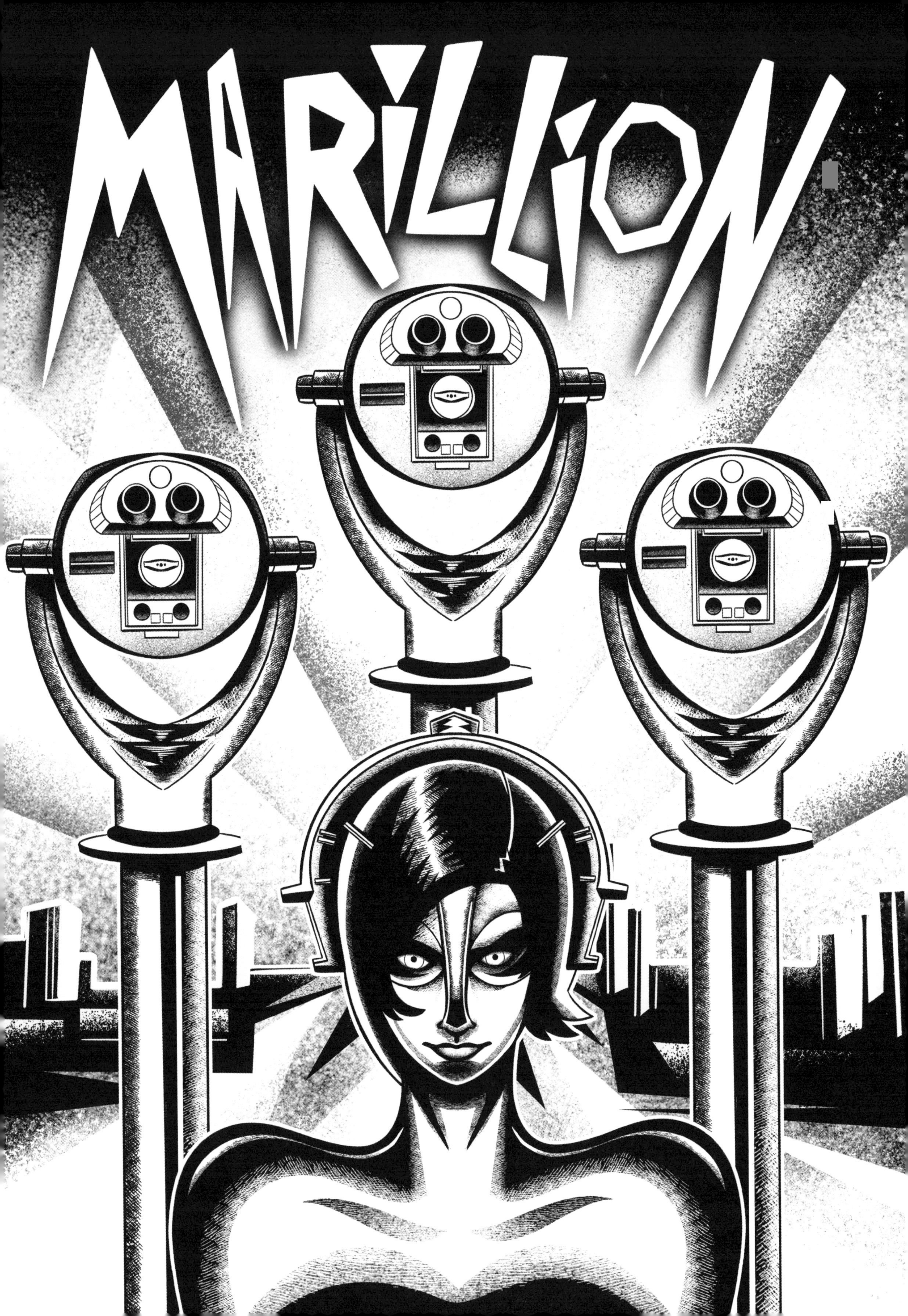
MARILLION

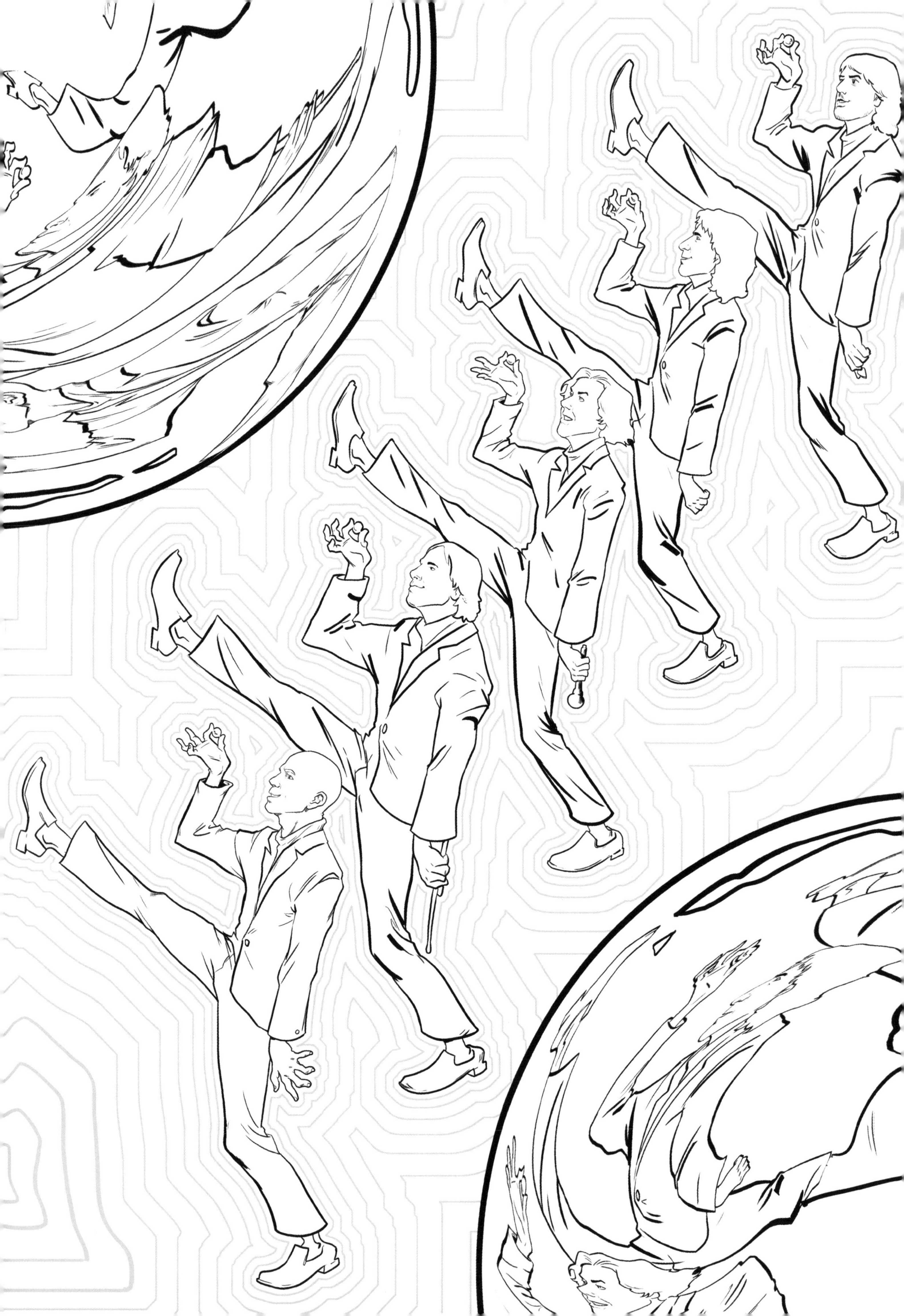